Japanese Identity

This volume is dedicated to Dr. Willie T. Nagai,
in deep appreciation for his contributions
to the study of Japan.

Number 2

Teikyo
Loretto
Heights
University

JAPAN STUDIES

Publications of the
Center for Japan Studies at
Teikyo Loretto Heights
University

*Linking the Minds
of the World*

JAPANESE IDENTITY:
CULTURAL ANALYSES

EDITED BY
PETER NOSCO

A publication of the Center for Japan Studies at Teikyo Loretto Heights University, Denver, Colorado. Although the Center is responsible for the selection and acceptance of manuscripts in the series, responsibility for the opinions expressed and for the accuracy of statements rests with the authors.

Distributed by
Institute of East Asian Studies Publications
University of California
2223 Fulton St., MC#2318
Berkeley, California 94720-2318
E-mail: easia@uclink.berkeley.edu

Library of Congress Cataloging-in-Publication Data

Japanese identity : cultural analyses / edited by Peter Nosco.
    p. cm. — (Japan studies ; no. 2)
    ISBN 0-9650254-1-1 (trade pbk.)
    1. Japan—Civilization—1868– 2. National characteristics, Japanese. I. Nosco, Peter. II. Series: Japan studies (Center for Japan Studies at Teikyo Loretto Heights University) ; no. 2.
DS822.25.J367 1997
952—dc20
                                                                       96-46565
                                                                         CIP

Copyright © 1997 by The Center for Japan Studies at Teikyo Loretto
   Heights University, Denver, Colorado.
Printed in the United States of America.
All rights reserved.

Contents

Contributors vi

Preface vii
        Kazuro Hanihara

Introduction: Cultural Analyses of Japanese Identity 1
        Peter Nosco

1. Geopolitics, Geoeconomics, and the Japanese Identity 10
        Harumi Befu

2. Biological Affinities of the Japanese Population 33
        Kazuro Hanihara

3. Autobiographical Writings by Tamura Toshiko and
   Miyamoto Yuriko 43
        Reiko Yonogi

4. Transforming Business Data into Literature:
   Shimizu Ikkō's *The Artery Archipelago* 54
        Tamae Prindle

5. The Identity in the Carpet 68
        Cris Reyns

6. Discernment or Volition: Linguistic Politeness Strategy
   in Japanese 83
        Shoji Azuma

8. The Interface of Two Cultural Constructs: *Kotodama*
   and *Fūdo* 96
        Ann Wehmeyer

9. Modern Roots in Ancient Traditions: Pilgrimage
   on Mount Fuji 107
        Erik L. Moore

Contributors

Shoji Azuma is Assistant Professor, Department of Languages and Literature, University of Utah.

Harumi Befu was Professor of Anthropology, Stanford University, at the time of the conference. Currently he is Professor of Cultural Anthropology and Director of the Institute for Cultural and Human Research at Kyoto Bunkyo University, Uji, Japan, and Professor Emeritus, Stanford University.

Kazuro Hanihara is Vice-Director, International Institute for Advanced Studies (Kyoto), and Professor Emeritus, University of Tokyo and International Center for Japanese Studies (Kyoto).

Erik Moore is Assistant Professor of Fine Arts at Teikyo Loretto Heights University.

Peter Nosco is Professor of East Asian Languages and Cultures, and History, University of Southern California.

Tamae Prindle is Associate Professor of Japanese Language and Literature, Colby College, and Chair of the East Asian Studies Department.

Cris Reyns is a Ph.D. student in Comparative Literature, University of Colorado at Boulder.

Ann Wehmeyer is Associate Professor of Japanese and Linguistics, Department of African and Asian Languages and Literatures, University of Florida, Gainesville, Florida.

Reiko Yonogi is Assistant Professor in Japanese Studies, Indiana University, Indianapolis.

Preface

KAZURO HANIHARA

For a majority of today's Japanese, one of the most frequently asked and difficult-to-answer questions is "What is Japanese identity?" Until recently, most Japanese people found it unnecessary to consider the question of their national identity, simply accepting that the Japanese people and their culture are unique because of their distinctive ethnicity and cultural tradition centered on the emperor.

After World War II, however, these myths of Japanese uniqueness were almost completely destroyed, and as a result many Japanese lost their sense of identity. To fill this void, there appeared on the stage a relativistic scientific-historical view of Japanese identity, stressing the importance of comparative studies of history and culture. This meant that Japanese had to find their identity by examining themselves in relation to different ethnic groups, cultural traditions, and ways of thinking.

The deep interest of ordinary Japanese people in Japan's ancient history and archaeology after the war is perhaps the reflection of this lost sense of identity. This interest is still booming, so that if one looks around the history section of any large bookstore in Japan, one will easily find hundreds of books on ancient history, archaeology, ethnology, anthropology, and so on, all written for the "amateur historian." This trend suggests that many Japanese are indeed still searching for their identity.

In this regard, the "Symposium on Japanese Identity: Cultural Analyses" held in April 1995 at the Center for Japan Studies at Teikyo Loretto Heights University was altogether timely and of special importance. Just as one can scarcely apprehend one's own personality in all its fullness, people can hardly analyze their identity objectively because it is virtually impossible to observe oneself from the perspective of another. International and intercultural discussions of identity are thus both fruitful and important.

In this symposium several different aspects of Japanese identity were examined by non-Japanese scholars and by Japanese scholars living outside Japan. Their methods were colorful and variegated, including such perspectives as those of social and cultural anthropology, traditional consciousness, sociolinguistics, literature, and so forth. All of these papers provide us with fresh perspectives on the subject of Japanese identity, perspectives that often differ somewhat from those offered by Japanese scholars living inside Japan.

Today, one finds a large number of institutes for Japan studies actively working throughout the world. However, the answer to the question "What is Japanese identity?" remains a subject worthy of investigation. Searching for the identity of a certain ethnic group may be an endless research subject, but this symposium undoubtedly represents a milestone in its contribution to this goal of Japanese studies.

Finally, I wish to express my deep indebtedness to Dr. Willie T. Nagai, director of the Center for Japan Studies, for inviting me to speak at this symposium. I am also grateful to Ms. Allison Crane, program coordinator, and the staff of the center for their superb organization of such an important academic event.

INTRODUCTION

Cultural Analyses of Japanese Identity

PETER NOSCO

Those who have studied or lived in Japan will likely agree that there are few, if any, (post)modern societies in which national identity is as compelling a subject of both scholarly and popular discussion as in Japan. The proliferation of books, magazine and newspaper articles, and talk-show discussions is such that it would not be an exaggeration to regard the subject of national identity as something of an industry. So strong is contemporary interest in the subject that one needs to be reminded that it has not always been so and that the concern—some would say *obsession*—with the subject of cultural and racial identity was not a meaningful topic in Japanese discourse before the Tokugawa period (1600–1868).

To be sure, there has long been on the part of those who have lived there an awareness of "Japan" as an entity with distinctive properties, and Japan's Shinto tradition is often identified as one of these properties. As is well known, the designation of Japan as the "land of the *kami*" (Shinto deities) or "divine land" (*shinkoku*) has its locus classicus in the *Nihon shoki* of 720 in which the king of the Korean kingdom of Silla is quoted: "I have heard that there is a divine land to the east and that it is called Nippon."[1] This appellation reappears during the classical Heian period (794–1185) in such texts as the *Sandai jitsuroku* and *Gyokuyō* and again in the medieval period in the *Tale of the Heike* (*Heike monogatari*), but it is in Kitabatake Chikafusa's (1293–1353) *Chronicle of Gods and Sovereigns* (*Jinnō shōtōki*) that one finds the term *shinkoku* first used explicitly to distinguish Japan from other lands on the basis of

---

[1] Translation adapted from W. G. Aston, *Nihongi: Chronicles of Japan from the Earliest Times to A.D. 697* (Rutland and Tokyo: Charles Tuttle Reprint, 1972), 1:230.

Japan's cultural tradition of belief in *kami* as an enduring numinous presence and benedictors of the polity: "Great Japan is the divine land. The heavenly progenitor founded it, and the sun goddess bequeathed it to her descendents to rule eternally. Only in our country is this true; there are no similar examples in other countries."[2] This focus on Shinto as a distinctively Japanese religious tradition came to be one component of the related argument that inasmuch as Confucianism and Buddhism have their roots in China and India respectively, Shinto is the solitary native creed or cultural "foundation" and hence part of what it means to be "Japanese."[3] One would be hard pressed, however, to find evidence of other cultural arguments before the Tokugawa period to support the premise that the people of Japan claimed a distinctive identity.

It is not until the second half of the seventeenth century that one finds a sustained scholarly discourse on Japanese identity. Ironically, the emergence of this concern appears to have been fostered by the new interest in Confucianism, which had its own traditions of ethnocentrism and scholarly inquiry into the past. These same tendencies reappear in their new Japanese setting with unprecedented vigor and are manifested in a variety of academic pursuits during the seventeenth century, when Japanese scholars sought to engage questions of the history of the polity. It remains the case, however, that before roughly the eighteenth century, serious interest in Japan was melded with the study of China into a singular discourse of scholarship (*gakumon*), in which Sinology was generally regarded as the weightier subject.

All this changed with the scholarship of those who were later styled *kokugakusha* or National Learning figures. The principal figures of the *kokugaku* lineage, and those sometimes referred to as its "great men," include the Buddhist monk Keichū (1640–1701), the Shinto priest and antiquarian researcher Kada no Azumamaro (1669–1736), the classicist Kamo no Mabuchi (1697–1769), the gifted literary critic and Shinto fundamentalist Motoori Norinaga (1730–1801), and the charismatic popularizer Hirata Atsutane (1776–1843). Their achievement was first to separate Japanese

---

[2] H. Paul Varley, trans., *A Chronicle of Gods and Sovereigns: Jinnō shōtōki of Kitabatake Chikafusa* (New York: Columbia University Press, 1980), p. 49.

[3] This argument persistently disregards the facts that both Confucianism and Buddhism arrived in Japan via Korea and that the religious practices of ancient Korea appear to have been virtually indistinguishable from those of Japan.

studies from the study of China and to endow the former with independent integrity; second, to establish a canon of Japanese literary and historical classics on which a curriculum of Japanese studies might be based (a canon and curriculum still commonly used in Japan); third, to use the methodology of historical linguistics to decipher certain ancient Japanese texts—most prominently the late-eighth-century *Man'yōshū* poetry anthology and the *Kojiki* history of 712—which had heretofore been inaccessible to contemporary readers; and fourth, to attempt to glean from these ancient classics what they believed to be a distinctive temperament and spirit that might form the nucleus for a native Japanese Way, in contrast to the imported and hence inferior Ways of Buddhism and Confucianism. This last effort heralds the concern with Japanese cultural identity that has become such a prominent feature in twentieth-century Japan.

In the first half of this century, discussions of Japanese identity shared much with their Tokugawa-period roots, since there was no attempt to veil arguments of Japanese racial and cultural superiority in the broader context of inquiry into the national past and character. The principal components supporting such xenophobic arguments were those used centuries earlier to argue similarly for Japan's distinctiveness: Japan's divine creation by Japanese *kami*; the divine institution and benediction of Japan's imperial polity and line; the endowment of Japanese persons with mind-hearts (*kokoro*) that differed from those of others less blessed; and an attendant sense of destiny concerning Japan's position in an Asian world order.

In the second half of the century following Japan's defeat in the Pacific War, arguments concerning Japan's racial and cultural superiority became something of a taboo topic, and attention shifted to such relatively "innocent" subjects as the untrue assertions that the origins of the Japanese people and language are mysterious (as if only one "people" speaking only one "language" has lived in Japan); broadly binary approaches to the culture and civilization (Ruth Benedict's *The Chrysanthemum and the Sword* would be just one example of many) in which the culture is represented as comprising apparently contradictory elements; and certain properties alleged to be essentially universal among Japanese people such as harmony, racial and cultural homogeneity, consensus decision making, love of and unique affinity for nature, and so on.

Discussions of Japanese identity thus tend by their very nature to be controversial and are fraught with altogether legitimate questions. Is there such a "thing" as national identity? If so, how is it to be defined, and where is it to be found? Can discussions of national identity be conducted without complicity with those ideological processes that have at times endorsed such discussions for (ultra)nationalistic purposes and with disastrous consequences? These are but a few of the questions that arise; others will no doubt occur to the thoughtful reader.

Recognizing both the problematic nature of these questions and the compelling and ongoing interest in this subject in Japan, a number of scholars gathered in April 1995 at the Center for Japan Studies at Teikyo Loretto Heights University in Denver for a two-day symposium on the theme (broadly defined) of cultural analyses of Japanese identity; the remainder of this volume is composed of papers delivered at that conference. They examine the question of Japanese identity at times critically, at times skeptically, and at times sympathetically, and they represent a variety of disciplinary approaches to the question: sociology, physical and social anthropology, linguistics, and studies of literature lie in the pages that follow. This introductory chapter is intended to introduce these chapters briefly and to create something of a context for their discussion.

Harumi Befu's essay, one of two keynote addresses at the symposium, analyzes the quest for national, racial, and cultural identity in Japan in terms of the current fascination with what is often styled *Nihonjinron*, or theories of Japaneseness. These include "the whole gamut of Japan's traditional cultural repository" and are often linked to articulations of Japanese cultural and racial superiority. Tracing this movement from its roots in the nativist discourse of *kokugaku* in the late-Tokugawa period and through its permutations during the nineteenth and twentieth centuries, Befu interprets *Nihonjinron* principally as a response to an external referent, which is to say that Japanese identity has been and continues to be framed largely in juxtaposition with an Other— represented by China during most of Japan's history and more recently "the West," meaning industrialized Europe and North America.

Befu identifies those intervals when Japan represented itself unfavorably vis-à-vis the external referent and contrasts them with those such as the present, when *Nihonjinron* represent Japan favorably in relation to an unfavorably depicted referent. Styling the former "negative self-identity," he regards it as a form of "auto-Orientalism (or 'do-it-to-yourself Orientalism')..., a process of accepting the 'Orientalism' of the West by the very people who are being Orientalized." During these intervals, the favorably constructed Other serves as both an implicit critique of Japan and a model for certain kinds of reform and transformation. The latter, in turn, represents those intervals when an essentialized Japan posits a world order in which Japan enjoys pride of place; it is fundamentally an optimistic and self-confident self-representation.

Kazuro Hanihara uses physical anthropology to shed light on the question of the racial origins of persons in Japan. Hanihara's "dual structure model," a theory for which he is well known both in and outside Japan, represents what may be the most compelling single explanation for the seemingly perennial questions of who the Japanese are and where they came from. Such questions are of course fundamental to any discussion of identity—be it for the macrocosm of the nation or the microcosm of the self—and as such, one might imagine that the answers Hanihara provides to these questions would be welcomed as the definitive resolution of a culturally knotty issue. Yet as popular as his analyses have proven (particularly in Japan), it is significant that the industry of cultural production that at once both invokes and mystifies such questions remains in high gear despite the persuasive theoretical contributions of Hanihara and his followers.

One possible explanation for this apparent paradox is that the narcissistic impulses that impel such levels of attention to questions of identity in Japan exist at least as much for the satisfaction derived from the pursuit of "answers" as they do from the "answers" themselves. Furthermore, Hanihara's analyses also point at times to conclusions that contradict officially sanctioned interpretations. For example, his observations concerning the cultural and physical diversity of Japan and its people are at odds with the remarkable societal emphasis on regarding Japanese people as racially homogenous, a perspective generated and reinforced by well over a century of ideological production in Japan.

Both Reiko Yonogi's and Tamae Prindle's essays deal with the search for female identity in the context of literary topics. As Reiko Yonogi points out, "Both self-discovery and the search for identity became main themes in literature not only in the West but also in Japan," and nowhere is this more evident than in Japanese literature of the last hundred or so years. Yonogi's essay focuses attention on the two women writers Tamura Toshiko (1884–1945) and Miyamoto Yuriko (1899–1951), whose writings, like those of many of their male contemporaries in the Japanese world of letters, have a strongly autobiographical component to them. As Yonogi indicates, "Their novels and short stories dramatize female characters' search for identity in modern society, and their works are united by a feminist consciousness."

In a process that obscures the distinction between author and character, text and context, both writers constructed narratives of female self-discovery that parallel the identity-creation experienced by the authors themselves. With the experience of art thus melded into the experience of life, one imagines the act of literary creation as one of catharsis in which female identity with feminist consciousness is literally fabricated out of words on paper.

Tamae Prindle's essay, the other keynote address at the symposium, looks at the genre of the business novel (*keizai shōsetsu*), in particular Shimizu Ikkō's 1974 business who-done-it *The Artery Archipelago* (*Dōmyaku rettō*), in which the Shinkansen train system becomes a metaphor for the human arterial system. Prindle posits a number of binary oppositions in her analysis of the novel. On the one hand are the Shinkansen itself, its administration and staff, a number of government ministers including the prime minister, the police, a psychologist consultant, and even the highly Sinified language of technical jargon, all subsumed under the rubric of masculinity. On the other hand are the Shinkansen's victims and their circle, which includes a bar hostess and an elderly female patient, collectively assigned the female voice of victimhood. These women, however, do not conform to the submissive stereotype, for in Prindle's words, they are neither "parasitic to men nor do they cater to the established political organizations." Instead, they represent the naturalistic, environmental, and decentralized periphery, in contrast to the technocratic, mechanical, and monolithically centralized realm of the masculine.

In Prindle's analysis, it is the male lawyer Akiyama Hiroshi who mediates between these realms, identifying with and representing the interests of the female victims—a veritable "guest of honor" in their camp—while using the presumably masculine traits of rebellion and even lawlessness. He is thus an androgynous traveler between the two realms, partaking of both but belonging wholly to neither. Prindle's analysis sheds light on the porous and permeable properties of the boundary between the seemingly sharply divided realms of male and female identity in Japan and suggests broader questions of whether victimhood in

Japan is necessarily framed in ways completely consistent with gendered identities.

Cris Reyns's essay, in turn, looks at Ibuse Masuji's *Black Rain*, a seminal work in the literature of the atomic bomb and an enduring best-seller regarded by many as the most important single work published in Japan since 1945. As in the essays by Yonogi and Prindle, here too one finds the issue of victimhood. No one would deny the importance of the events of 1945 in Hiroshima and Nagasaki in shaping the identity of succeeding generations of postwar Japanese, and yet nagging issues remain. Might one regard the victims of Hiroshima and Nagasaki as twice victimized: first by the events of 1945 in all their horror and second by the manipulation of public opinion on the issue of nuclear victimhood by a succession of governments unwilling or unable to represent the events of 1945 in their broader historical context? Such manipulation denies the victims of nuclear attack and their latter-day memorializers an opportunity for reconciliation with an excruciatingly painful legacy; the injustice to them thus goes on and contributes anew with each generation to the formation of an identity of victimhood.

At the symposium, several papers engaged topics and issues related to the study of linguistics. That language is fundamental to culture is obvious: just as one's perspectives are shaped by the language in which those perspectives are constructed and articulated, likewise the world one inhabits makes demands upon one's language to more effectively express that which requires expression. Similarly, learning a new language is akin to entering a gateway to a new realm, as suggested by the Czech saying (loosely paraphrased) that "as many languages as one knows, so many times is one a human being."[4]

Shoji Azuma's essay examines the question of linguistic politeness. That the Japanese language appears better suited than, say, American English for the precise expression of relative status is generally accepted, though some would question whether this difference has not been to some extent overstated. Such reservations notwithstanding, Azuma's essay demonstrates that speakers of Japanese make such distinctions in the context of politeness with greater precision than do speakers of English. The essay is also suggestive of that exquisite transformation that occurs when, for example, a native speaker of American English is speaking

---

[4] Variations of this saying can of course be found in any number of languages.

Japanese, and vice versa. As one enters the alternative linguistic realm, one is both transported and transformed in ways that appropriate far more cultural context than simply linguistic convention.

Ann Wehmeyer's essay, in turn, sheds light on questions of "typical Japanese characteristics" by examining how cultural historians in Japan have themselves focused on *kotodama* (word spirit) and *fūdo* (climate) in their construction of theories of Japaneseness. The belief that there is an abiding and mysterious power in words is evident in Japanese texts as early as the eighth century, and linguistically oriented nativists of the eighteenth century offered numerous explanations for the phenomenon. Wehmeyer argues that "depending on the historical period, 'word spirit' has been viewed as unique to the Japanese language, and when thus construed, it constitutes part of the ideology of the 'theory of Japanese uniqueness,' or *Nihonjinron*: the investigation of the cultural characteristics of the Japanese people that distinguish them from peoples of other countries and civilizations." Similarly, the belief that Japan is distinguished from other countries by its four seasons is a premise with antecedents in texts dating from at least the tenth century; in the last century it received its most comprehensive expression in the writings of Watsuji Tetsurō (1889–1960) and his disciples. Such theories of climatism form a prominent part of present-day articulations of Japanese uniqueness, and Wehmeyer identifies two areas in present-day Japan in which one may observe vestiges of *fūdo* arguments: "The first is the tendency of cultural critics to focus on Japan as a land of 'four seasons,' and therefore, it is argued, to engender a culture that is more variegated, on the one hand, and more able to adopt, on the other, various alien cultural practices that may then be modified for application to the Japanese context.... The second area is in the promotion of regionally based production as superior, or what may be called a type of national product fetishism." The arguments concerning a distinctive climate in Japan are of course related to the notions of a distinctive Japanese affinity with nature and to conceptions of national benediction and destiny.

The quest for identity in Japan may be thought of as having a twofold character: on the one hand, it is akin to a pilgrimage in which one seeks to learn about oneself and, ironically, in the process to become transformed; on the other hand, it has the character of a mission, in which one seeks to share what one has learned with others, that they might be similarly transformed. Erik

Moore's essay, which concludes this volume, is about the process of transformation he experienced in that quintessentially Japanese experience, an ascent of Mt. Fuji.

Moore sought to find the "right way" to perform the pilgrimage by studying the traditions of the ascent as it had been performed in earlier times. In the process of emulating these traditions in the present, he came to the conclusion that his goal of "climbing Fujisan the 'right way' was not possible, not because the traditional shrines have fallen into ruin, but because there is no one right way.... The only 'right way' I would find on the mountain would be the 'right way for me at that time.'" The quest for identity through pilgrimage is thus necessarily individualized, even as it is subsumed in patterns with a collective character.

That an American might seek to follow a Japanese tradition and thereby gain insight and personal growth is, of course, no less remarkable than that a Japanese might do the same with some feature of American culture, and in his remarkably personal testimony, Moore interestingly arrives at conclusions similar to those of Takuji Masuda, who joined an international "safari" of traditional longboard surfers with the intention of documenting his trek so that "perhaps young Japanese surfers would begin to see the beauty of classical longboard surfing." Masuda's observations upon the conclusion of his "safari" provide a counterpoint to those of Moore:

> By the end of our trip, we all felt fortunate to have met such wonderful people, and to have been treated so openly by them. I felt as though there was this natural tendency for the longboarders to pass on knowledge, and to keep the old stories and history alive.... The most important thing we learned on our mission is that we are always on the road, and the road never ends. As young monks, we must stay on the path, looking for truth.[5]

The quest for identity is inevitably an intensely personal quest, even if the venture is collectivized by the pursuit of a posited national type. At the national level, this may well be an exercise in "auto-Orientalism," to invoke Harumi Befu's marvelously apt term, and yet the quest does at times provide meaning and attendant solace; and if not meaning, then at least an interpretive context to help one orient oneself on the path.

---

[5] *Longboard Magazine* 3, 5 (December/January 1995/96): 69, 73.

ONE

Geopolitics, Geoeconomics, and the Japanese Identity

HARUMI BEFU

The contemporary discourse on Japan's national cultural identity takes place in the genre of *Nihonjinron*, otherwise called *Nihonron*, *Nihon bunkaron*, and the like. In this discourse, Japan's uniqueness is argued in terms of the gamut of Japan's traditional cultural repository, including values, language, social institutions, and mental disposition. These characteristics not only make Japan unique, but also inform Japan's cultural sophistication, such as in art and literature, and constitute the "cultural infrastructure" for Japan's economic success. Decision by consensus, hierarchical organization, and group-orientation are but a few of the characteristics that constitute the contents of this identity.

The nature of this identity, however, has not been the same throughout the history of Japan. In this essay I deal with the complexity of these differing identities in different periods. This brief review of the vicissitudes of Japan's identity discourse is attempted not so much for the intrinsic interest in the history of Japan's identity discourse as such, but to ask what external factors have affected changing definitions of national identity. It is my thesis that national identity is a creature living very much in adaptation to its external environment.[1] It should be noted at the outset that we are relying on the writings of intellectuals of the

---

This paper, shortened and revised from Befu 1995, is based on the research conducted at the East-West Center, Honolulu, Hawaii, where I held a fellowship from September 1991 to March 1992. The center's support is gratefully acknowledged. Thanks are due Nancy Stalker for her excellent editorial work.

Japanese personal names in the text are written in accordance with the Japanese convention of showing the family name first, followed by the given name.

[1] For the history of *Nihonjinron* see Aoki (1989), Ikumatsu (1963), and Minami (1980).

time for the understanding of the nature of national and cultural identity. To what extent ordinary Japanese "on the street" espoused the same views as those expressed by intellectuals is a totally separate issue, which I cannot deal with here.[2]

Nascent Nativism in the Late Tokugawa Period

Understanding contemporary *Nihonjinron* and its historical lineage takes us back at least to the late eighteenth and early nineteenth century, or the late Tokugawa period. Already in the late Tokugawa we find clear and definite discussion of self-identity of the Japanese. We see budding *Nihonjinron*, though it was not called that in those days, in the so-called *kokugaku* (national learning) school of scholarship.[3]

Kokugaku arose in reaction against the received Sinology emphasizing neo-Confucianism of the time, which heavily influenced the shogunate and daimiate feudal governments in formulating the official political and moral philosophy. In contrast, *kokugaku* emphasized and lauded virtues of what *kokugaku* scholars, such as Kamo no Mabuchi (1697–1769) and Motoori Norinaga (1730–1801), considered to be pure, indigenous Japanese characteristics, including the Japanese imperial institution and Japan's aesthetic values, such as *mono no aware* (melancholy). In *Shōikō*, Mabuchi openly criticized the effeminate China and in contrast raved about Japanese masculinity (*masurao*). When Norinaga pointed to fragrant cherry blossoms seen against the rising sun as the essence of the ethos of Japan (*yamato-gokoro*), juxtaposed with *kara-gokoro* (the ethos of China), he was definitely staking a claim of a Japan totally different from China and of the superiority of Japanese culture over Chinese culture. Norinaga also declared in *Kenkyōjin* that the sun goddess, Amaterasu, stood at the pinnacle of the world.

---

[2] Those interested in this issue may consult results of the questionnaire survey conducted by Manabe Kazufumi and me (Befu, McConnell, Kweon, and Manabe 1988; Manabe and Befu 1989; Manabe and Befu 1991).

[3] Intellectual history of the Tokugawa period is masterfully treated by such scholars as Harootunian (1988) and Nosco (1990). What I present here is mere surface-skimming of intensively investigated scholarship.

Kokugaku is indeed "an astonishingly complex" field of study, as Peter Nosco reminds us in his comment on this essay. I can hardly do justice to this complex field in this brief summary, which serious students of *kokugaku* would no doubt regard as gross simplification. I can only suggest the reader consult sources such as those above for more extended discussions.

It is important that Norinaga originally studied neo-Confucianism: his specialization in *kokugaku* was in personal reaction to and negation of that philosophy.[4] In attempting to demonstrate the superiority of Japanese culture over its referent culture—China—*kokugaku* scholars already manifested some of the same characteristics of modern *Nihonjinron* writers who try to prove Japan's superiority over the West.[5]

The fundamental fault of the Tokugawa regime, as far as the National Learning school was concerned, was that the shogun displaced the emperor as the rightful sovereign ruler of the country. The imperial system was a primordial institution indigenous to Japan. There was no way to rectify the situation except by toppling the Tokugawa regime and replacing it with the emperor system. For the National Learning school, Japan's highest virtues were to be sought in traditional Japan, unencumbered by any Chinese influence whatsoever. Hegemony of neo-Confucianism in Japanese polity was an unfortunate as well as erroneous twist in history from which Japan had to be rescued by putting indigenous institutions and values back at center stage where they once were and where they rightfully belonged. *Kokugaku*, then, was a nascent *Nihonjinron* that arose to compete with the dominant identity discourse based on Confucianism.

Discourse on Japan's national identity was and is directed at the foreign culture perceived to be the most significant for Japan for the moment, whether in military, political, or economic terms. In the Tokugawa period, this foreign culture was China, as it had given Japan much of its "high culture," such as Buddhism, artistic and architectural styles, and writing system. In post-Tokugawa Japan, the foreign culture has been the West. Thus the post-Tokugawa national identity discourse has had to contrast Japan with the West. Japan's relation to China in this regard became secondary and less relevant.

---

[4] It reminds one of Watsuji Tetsurō, who a hundred years later was to write *Fūdo*, after returning from his study of Western philosophy in Germany, in reaction to Western philosophers' theory of the relationship between nature and human beings (Watsuji 1935).

[5] Minami, in his history of *Nihonjinron*, points out (1980:84), however, that Norinaga had in mind a pan-human feeling when he spoke about *mono no aware*, rather than a uniquely Japanese quality. Just as Western scholars create what they consider to be universal concepts out of their own Western intellectual experience, Norinaga was doing the same.

But this was not a sudden shift. From the end of the eighteenth century, black ships of Western powers, one after another, began to appear off the coast of Japan, demanding through their "gunboat diplomacy" that Japan open its ports for trading. Hard as Japan tried to ward off the "hairy barbarians," Western military might proved too much for the very best swords of Japan and even for the *tanegashima* firearms that the Japanese had obtained from the Portuguese in the sixteenth century. As a result, Japan experienced the humiliation of being forced to give up its self-imposed seclusion and having to sign treaties with terms unfavorable to itself. The shame of this "symbolic rape" was too much for Japanese political leaders to endure. It was indelibly imprinted on them, and it defined Japanese attitudes toward the West for the next 140 years.

This geopolitics of shame led the impatient *shishi*, the "samurai with purpose" of a National Learning persuasion, to take a competing stance against the shogunate and to challenge its legitimacy by proclaiming the legitimacy of the (for all intents and purposes deposed) emperor on the basis of the latter's primordial legacy.

The late Tokugawa period was, then, characterized by these two competing forces, one propounding neo-Confucianism, which was used to legitimate the Tokugawa shogunate, and the other placing the emperor at center stage and regarding neo-Confucianism as inauthentic and the shogunate supported by it as illegitimate. In the end *kokugaku's* basic tenets held sway and led to the collapse of the regime that was supported by the rival ideology of neo-Confucianism. The new Meiji regime, however, did not do away with Confucianism but instead combined it with central elements of *kokugaku*, creating a new imperial institution.

This phenomenon of Japan imbued with overwhelmingly positive valuation and negative Other (China, in the Tokugawa period) was to be repeated in Japanese history—during the late Meiji; from around 1930 to the end of World War II; and most recently, during the last fifteen to twenty years.

Auto-Orientalism in the Meiji Period

To come to terms with the military and technological gap with the West that Japan was forced to recognize, Meiji leaders ushered in a frenzied period of catch-up through borrowing and adapting Western technology and institutions in an effort to bring not only

Japan's military strength but its political, economic, educational, and other institutions up to par with those of the West.

This situation necessitated that Japan develop a new definition of itself vis-à-vis the West. China was no longer a nation to contend with. The question Who are the Japanese? became What makes Japan different from the West? From facing west toward China, Japan turned 180 degrees, to facing east toward the United States and Europe. Now Japan's identity had to contain elements to distinguish it from the West.

Fukuzawa Yukichi, Nishi Amane, and other intellectuals wrote in the second half of the last century comparing Japan with the West and argued the pros and cons of Japanese culture. In a pseudonymously authored article, Fukuzawa contrasted Japanese character with Western character and listed those character traits in which Westerners were supposedly superior and those in which Westerners were inferior (Minami 1980:116–117). Among the former were independence, cooperation, perseverance, ability to take care of assets swiftly, and valuing of trust. Among the latter were excessive pitying of women leading to excessive respect of them, arrogance of women, forgetting one's station in life, and neglecting ethical considerations because of a desire to accumulate wealth. These may also be seen as what Fukuzawa perceived to be the flip side of the Japanese character traits.

Fukuzawa was radical in advocating changes to the Japanese character. In particular, he despised what he regarded as an outmoded "feudal" mentality among the Japanese. This view of denigrating the Japanese character by upholding European character and contrasting it with the Japanese was supported by a number of other intellectuals who belonged to a progressive organization called Meirokusha.[6] Many others took Japanese traditional values and institutions to task, some even advocating mixed marriage with Europeans as a way of infusing Caucasian blood to improve the Japanese race, according to Minami (1980:25).

The overwhelming mood of the time was that Japanese technology and social institutions were hopelessly outmoded and needed to be replaced by the more advanced Western technology and institutions. The zeal with which the Japanese absorbed Western civilization was phenomenal. It went far beyond guns and boats. Western costume was declared the official attire for

---

[6] This self-denigration was to be repeated, almost in carbon copy, in the immediate post-WWII period.

government employees. Things of Western origin, whether food, shelter, or clothing, enjoyed high prestige. This infatuation with Western civilization ushered in the "Rokumeikan period," so called because of a Western-style "society" building called Rokumeikan in the middle of Tokyo, where the members of high society competed in displaying how Westernized they were, showing off their Western clothes and their skills in Western social manners and ballroom dancing.

The Japanese language, that sacrosanct store of the essence of Japanese spirit according to National Learning scholars, lost its raison d'être for some of the Meiji thinkers. According to Minami (1980:110–111), Nishi Amane, one of the foremost thinkers of the time, even advocated in 1874 using the English alphabet (*yōji*) to record Japanese (*wago*), anticipating Mori Arinori's similar but more extreme proposal only a few years later. Mori, one of the intellectual leaders of the Meiji period and a one-time minister of education, suggested abolishing Japanese and replacing it with English.[7]

The Japanese did not arrive at this conclusion alone. Most Westerners who came to Japan to teach Japanese Western technology and to help build institutions modeled after those in the West, such as banking, the military, and education, assumed that Japan was a backward country needing the enlightenment of the West. Western scientists, engineers, and scholars came to Japan in droves, taking high-paying salaries no Japanese of equivalent position could possibly earn, and showed Japanese how to become modernized. The willingness of the Japanese government to pay such high salaries to foreigners showed the political leadership's admission of Japan's backwardness. In the end, however, Western cultural emulation during the Meiji was superficial in many respects, costume parties at Rokumeikan being a metaphor for the superficiality of the Western cultural cloak that Meiji socialites and elites wore, as Uchida Roan wrote in 1916 assessing the so-called Rokumeikan period (Uchida 1968).

I propose to call this process "auto-Orientalism" (or "do-it-to-yourself Orientalism"). It is a process of accepting the "Orientalism" of the West (Said 1978) by the very people who are being Orientalized. Psychologically a masochistic process, it signifies internalization by the Orientalized people of the observation and judgment by the West toward them. Said, of course, focused on

---

[7] See Miller (1982:107–109) for the circumstances surrounding this suggestion.

the Middle East for the Orientalized people, but a similar Orientalizing process took place in other parts of the world, including Japan (Kang 1988, Minear 1980, Mouer 1983), where the Japanese accepted the Western-centric scheme of the universe and believed in Westerners' value judgments about Japan's backwardness.

As far as basic human substance was concerned, however, the Japanese believed then—as they do now—that they had what it took spiritually to transform Japan into a modern nation. *Wakon yōsai*, meaning "Japanese spirit, Western know-how," was the motto of the day, appropriately modified from the older motto, *wakon kansai*, meaning "Japanese spirit, Chinese know-how." The West replaced China as the role model for Japan.

But one cannot say that the discourse on national identity of the day had a mass following in the way *Nihonjinron* has now. Concern with Japan's identity vis-à-vis the West was a minor issue for the Japanese population as a whole, even though, to be sure, it was the few economically powerful men and women—those who made the difference for Japan's future—who concerned themselves with the issue of who the Japanese were. We should not lose sight of the contrast in numbers and proportions of those engaged, actively or passively, in this identity discourse then and now. It was only after WWII that identity discourse became a concern of the masses. Until then, a relatively small, though increasing, number of people were involved in this discourse.

It is important that from the beginning of Meiji, the feeling of inferiority was firmly implanted as a result of gunboat diplomacy. Fukuzawa was particularly harsh on Japan and criticized it while lauding the West. For these individuals Western culture was all-powerful; Japanese culture represented backwardness to be abandoned and forgotten. The slogan of the day, *bummei kaika*, meaning "flowering of civilization," referred to adopting Western civilization as a means of developing Japan. Love and admiration of the West continued as the manifest modus vivendi.

Return of Positive Identity

Yet one should not conclude that during the Meiji period the intellectual outlook was totally oriented toward degrading Japan. Far from it, as demonstrated in the volume edited by Sakata Yoshio (1958) on Japan's nationalism in the early and middle—but mostly middle—Meiji period. Perhaps partly in reaction to excessive Western devotion, mid-Meiji saw the appearance of periodicals such as *Nihon* (1889–) and *Nihonjin* (1888–), whose mission was to reawaken the Japanese people to uniquely Japanese characteristics and thereby bolster the feeling of national pride and extol the virtues of Japan by publishing ultra-right-wing articles (Motoyama 1958).

This position received a major boost in 1890 with the promulgation of the Imperial Rescript on Education, which officially defined the mythologically founded emperor system and outlined the fundamental principles that were to govern the Japanese educational system for the next fifty-five years—until the defeat of Japan in the Pacific War. This event officially crystallized the pro-Japanese, positive discourse on Japanese identity. This imperial message is a curious mixture of traditional Japanese virtues and Confucian moral values. Although the centrality of the imperial institution was affirmed, the Confucian five relations were also given a position of importance in the education of the Japanese. In the rescript, the Japanese family system was presented as the embodiment of virtues and the foundation of the Japanese nation. The emperor was the father figure for the subjects. Social values such as *on* (one's indebtedness to others) and filial piety were said to have created a social order unequaled around the world. This imperial message unquestionably remained the most influential document for propagation of the hegemonic ideology of the time and for officially defining the Japanese identity.

Winston Davis (1976) has analyzed the commentaries that Inoue Tetsujirō, a Tokyo University professor, wrote on the Imperial Rescript, wherein Inoue propounded on the national morality as derived from Shinto—the indigenous religion translated as "the way of the gods"—and tied it in with the imperial institution and the concept of national polity (Inoue 1891). Although an army of others also wrote commentaries on the Imperial Rescript, Inoue was one of the most influential of the time. He successfully exploited his prestigious academic position to spread his ideas.

Inoue was one of the most ardent nationalists of the mid-Meiji. When the controversy erupted over whether foreigners should be allowed to live in Japan in intermingled residence with Japanese, he was moved to write from Berlin to voice his opposition. He feared racial contamination, which, according to him, would result in loss of the ability of the Japanese to work together, in physiological alterations of the Japanese, and possibly in the extinction of the Japanese race. This view contrasts sharply with the early Meiji view advocating mixed marriage for eugenic purposes.

That the Imperial Rescript on Education and also a good deal of *Nihonjinron* of the time contained many Confucian-derived ideas, such as the five principles of human ethics, may seem contradictory, if *Nihonjinron*'s goal were to identify pure, unadulterated, indigenous Japanese qualities. But *Nihonjinron*'s objective is otherwise: it is to distinguish Japan culturally from politically, economically, and militarily significant referent nations, which then were those of the West, and no longer China. The incorporation of Chinese or Confucian values, especially as nativized by Japanese neo-Confucian scholars, was therefore not seen as a problem in defining what constituted Japaneseness.[8]

By the late Meiji, as Japan's industrialization proceeded successfully and as Japan was slowly able to gain a stronger position vis-à-vis the West in diplomacy, trade issues, and military matters, the affirmative view of Japan began to hold sway. Japan was launching its own imperialist expansion into the continent and fighting back incursions by Western powers into East Asia. To rationalize Japan's action and to bolster Japanese morale, it was imperative to develop a national identity that made Japanese people feel proud of themselves. With the successive victories in the Sino-Japanese War of 1894–1895 and the Russo-Japanese War of 1904–1905, Japanese people were in a mood to accept such a self-definition. Although these wars crippled Japan's economy, the victories vastly enhanced Japan's international position. The improving self-image of Japan and the ascendancy of positive *Nihonjinron* should be seen in this geopolitical light.

As one might surmise, *Nihonjinron* of this time was imbued with nationalism. In fact the two were not separable. To laud and praise the ethnic essence of Japan was to sacralize the emperor and the nation. There was no better way of accomplishing this objective than to co-opt the indigenous folk Shinto and upgrade it to state Shintoism by placing the imperial institution at the center of this primordial, quintessentially Japanese religion and to formally organize hitherto private Shinto shrines into a hierarchy of state Shinto ecclesia. Creation of state Shintoism (Hardacre 1989, Holtom 1963), in short, was achieved by embracing, encompassing, and comprehending folk Shinto—so integral to

---

[8] This is a point that Dale (1986:59–60) misses in his critique of *Nihonjinron*.

essentialized "Japanliness"—under the state umbrella. Inasmuch as folk Shinto constituted an underpinning of *Nihonjinron*, appropriation of this *Nihonjinron*-in-private-sector for state purposes was a strategic move.

Shiga Shigekata, a political economist who contributed much to the magazine *Nihonjin* on Japan's economic policy, also wrote on uniquely Japanese characteristics. In creating his version of *Nihonjinron*, Shiga (1976, originally 1894) wrote a piece claiming Japan's natural scenery to be the most beautiful in the world, deriving from it a positively characterized Japanese personality. Miyake Setsurei (1977, originally 1891), another frequent contributor to *Nihonjin*, was more evenhanded in his view of the Japanese, enumerating both their ugly, seamy side and their laudable side. Miyake criticized Japan's "feudal class structure" and certain other facets but nevertheless did not advocate wholesale adoption of Western culture. Rather, he also praised Japan's traditional culture. Miyake's efforts were in reaction to the excessive Westernization of Japan and were supported by the ground swell to ameliorate the unequal treaties Japan had had to sign with Western powers.

By the late Meiji, intellectuals expressing positive views of Japan were legion. Ōmachi Keigetsu wrote much on the incomparable virtues of Japan. In the area of aesthetics, Minami notes Kitamura Tōkoku, who in 1891 elaborated on the aesthetic concept of *iki* (chic)—which had to do with the aesthetic value of the plebeian culture that developed in the Tokugawa period—in his review of Ozaki Kōyō's *Kyara makura*, anticipating Kuki's classic study (Kuki 1930) of the same concept (Minami 1980:90). These views of Japan expressed by intellectuals are consonant with the manifest ideology that crystallized in the late Meiji (Gluck 1985, Pyle 1969). Kamishima (1990:1) calls this late Meiji period "the first phase" of the Japanese concern with national identity.

Taisho Interlude

During the so-called Taisho democracy, liberal thinking pervaded Japan. There were some like Tanaka Yoshitau (1924), who wrote a very successful nationalistic book, reprinted six times in three years, on "national morality." His writings are reminiscent of Inoue Tetsujirō's in that the Imperial Rescript on Education is the centerpiece of his argument about "human conduct," which according to Tanaka is manifested in Shinto, bushido, familism, and loyalty to the nation.

But basically the Taisho period did not promise, promote, or encourage strong continuation of *Nihonjinron*. Virtually all of the thousands of foreign engineers, technicians, and scholars brought over to create a Westernized Meiji had been sent back by the end of Meiji. This was a time of relative peace in Japan. The liberalism of the Taisho period, though rooted in Western thought, was no longer obsessed with wholesale and uncritical absorption of Western culture, as was the case during the Rokumeikan period in the Meiji, but was more reflective and selective, assessing and evaluating things Western before importing them. Western thought, in fact, began to take root now; enlightenment and progressivism became more than the facade they had been in the Meiji period. Thus there was little room for staunchly nationalistic *Nihonjinron* to hold sway. Kamishima's periodization of *Nihonjinron*—though he does not call it that—skips the whole Taisho era and begins the second phase in the early Showa (Kamishima 1990:1).

Ultranationalism of the 1930s to 1945

In the 1930s we see the resurgence of patriotic *Nihonjinron* of the basic variety we saw in the late Meiji period. As Gluck (1985) says, Meiji ideologues laid the foundation of political thinking that was to continue until 1945. Rhetoric familiar from the late Meiji was repeated ever more fervently at this time: the emperor as the father figure for Japan's subjects and the Japanese family system as the embodiment of virtues and the foundation of the Japanese nation. Social values such as *on* and *giri* (social obligation) created a social order unequaled around the world. This self-praise, often in the form of unqualified ethnocentrism, increased in the 1930s when frenzied claims began to be made of the superiority of the Japanese in comparison with Europeans and Americans.

It was in the early Showa that Watsuji wrote his *Fūdo* (a classic in *Nihonjinron*), which sees an inextricable relationship between Japan's environment and its culture. As Minami (1980) notes, this publication was precipitated by the rise of Marxism. It was to answer Marxism by demonstrating the impossibility of accounting for Japanese culture in the framework of historical materialism.

About the same time, Kuki (1930), resuscitating Kitamura Tōkoku's argument but further enhancing it, wrote his famed treatise on the aesthetic concept of *iki* as representing the quintessential aesthetic value of the plebeian Japan. It is significant that Kuki's writing came after a decade of study in France, as Watsuji's came after his sojourn in Germany (Minami 1980:94–95).

Shirayanagi Shūko (1938), in his treatise on the Japanese people and nature, also argued the role of the environment in creating Japanese culture. Japanese environment, according to him, was the best and most desirable in the world and was even responsible for creating a uniquely Japanese genetic lineage (*kettō*) at the confluence of the continental culture and the oceanic culture; thus Shirayanagi conflated environment, culture, and biology, as is often the case in *Nihonjinron*. As Watsuji did in his treatises on ethics, Shirayanagi devoted much space to the mythological creation of the Japanese nation and founding of the emperor system. Even Nishida Kitarō, arguably the foremost philosopher Japan has ever produced and professor of Kyoto University, joined the ranks of nationalists by claiming that the essence of the Japanese spirit lay in the centrality of the imperial institution (Nishida 1940).

If the Imperial Rescript on Education was the most canonical of all canons of *Nihonjinron* before 1945, *Kokutai no hongi* (The Japanese polity), issued by the Ministry of Education in 1937 and distributed in large quantities, was one of the most canonical of the war-period *Nihonjinron* documents. This work elaborated on the centrality of the imperial institution in Japan and also argued that the Japanese nation and its people were unparalleled in the world. Although there was no explicit comparison with other nations, the intent was clearly to demonstrate the superiority of Japan over its real and imagined enemies in Asia and the West and to convince the Japanese people that therefore Japan was destined to win the war and rule the world. Numerous versions of its commentary were published and reprinted to meet the high demand.

Even Hasegawa Nyozekan, that spokesman of Taisho liberalism, in 1938 wrote *Nihon-teki seikaku* (The "Japanly" character), extolling what he argued to be specifically "Japanly" virtues. His argument is reminiscent of Watsuji's ecological theory, starting with the supposed effect of the geography of Japan upon its culture and extending into lifestyle, human relations, and art.

Japanese art, according to him, is not isolated and divorced from nature, as Western art—like a framed painting in a museum—supposedly is. Instead it is an integral part of nature, as seen in the Japanese garden and home. Hasegawa spoke of the refined sensitivity of the Japanese mind.

Suzuki Daisetz' *Zen to Nihon bunka* (Zen and Japanese culture) (1940) also appeared about this time, in wartime Japan, with endorsement by none other than Nishida Kitarō himself. Suzuki reviewed the influence of Zen in Japanese art, the ethics of warriors, Japanese Confucianism, the tea ceremony, and haiku, demonstrating the uniqueness of Japanese arts and aesthetics as influenced by Zen.

Examples can be adduced ad infinitum, but the above discussion is sufficient to demonstrate the ethnocentric and nationalistic nature of the *Nihonjinron* of the time. An important characteristic of that *Nihonjinron* is that in one form or another it became part of the official ideology in this period. It became part of the war propaganda of the government and was preached to, broadcast to, and forced upon people. The government used every means possible to propagate this worldview, including educational institutions and newspapers. It used secret police to almost totally shut out alternative and rival views, notably Marxism. This effort reached its height during World War II, and the bloated view that Japan in every respect was superior to the rest of the world continued until August 1945.

It may have looked as though all of Japan was spouting some version of *Nihonjinron* during the frenetic period of wartime—though no doubt in varying degrees of conviction or disbelief. But the view of Japan as backward, behind the West, and needing infusion of ideas from the West never completely died from early Meiji. Even at the height of government thought-control, according to Ikumatsu (1963:21–22), some, like Sakada Ango, were able openly to deny significance to Japanese tradition, as in the March 1942 issue of *Gendai bungaku*, where Sakada maintained that convenience is important in life. If chairs and tables proved to be more convenient than Japanese floor mats, so be it; one need not apologize for adopting Western conveniences. I recall my own middle-school principal publicly admiring the Allied leaders—Roosevelt, Churchill, Stalin, and Chiang Kai-shek—for staying in office throughout the war to provide consistent leadership and criticizing the Japanese government for the frequent turnover of its leadership.

Postwar Auto-Orientalism

In the immediate postwar era, disastrous defeat in the Pacific War meant not only military defeat but total devaluation of Japanese cultural values. For at least a decade, perhaps two decades, after 1945, Japan entered a period of depressing soul-searching. With the nation vanquished, the idealized *Nihonjinron* valorizing traditional values seemed worthless. If they were worth anything, why did Japan lose the war? Japanese people were promised victory by virtue of Japan's superior culture. The culture that was supposed to lead Japan to victory and conquest of the world failed to accomplish its mission. Traditional Japanese values and institutions, which were mobilized for fighting the war, were all now objects of criticism. "Feudalistic," "premodern," "outmoded," and "backward" were some of the epithets thrown at whatever represented old and traditional Japan.

Indeed, even the legitimacy and prestige of the emperor system were now in doubt (Befu 1992). After all, the emperor went to the headquarters of the Supreme Commander of the Allied Powers to pay homage to General Douglas MacArthur, rather than summoning MacArthur to the imperial palace for an audience. Newspapers carried on their front pages a huge picture of the six-foot-tall leader of the Occupation force, who was now often referred to as Japan's new emperor, towering over the diminutive emperor. More than words, this picture served to convince the Japanese that their emperor no longer was the kingpin of the Japanese polity. The imperial institution with its mythic foundation, national ideology, and symbolism, all of which were marshaled forth for the war effort and constituted the core of *Nihonjinron*, lost its venerable and revered status.

The Japanese family system was now to be condemned for its "feudal" character, as argued in the influential writings of Kawashima Takeyoshi (1950, 1957). The normative values of *on* and *giri* likewise were given negative scores. Japan's traditional virtues all were cast as vices. Before and during the war, wartime propagandists who contrasted democracy and individualism with Japanese values denigrated the former as worthless simply because they contrasted with what Japan had and valued. But with the military reversal, democracy was "in" and any Japanese institution and cultural value that contradicted or contrasted with democracy was "out" because the latter were by definition the cause of the defeat, according to the now fashionable postwar interpretation.

Even the Japanese language, the supposed storehouse of Japanese values and virtues according to prewar and wartime *Nihonjinron* advocates from Motoori Norinaga on, could not remain free from attack: Japanese afforded no logical discourse, according to its critics, as European languages presumably did. It enabled discourse in feeling and emotion only. Shiga Naoya, a well-known writer who was called "a god of fiction writing" for his literary facility, in 1946 even went so far as to resuscitate Mori Arinori's suggestion of fifty years earlier to abolish Japanese and replace it with a Western language, such as French (Miller 1982:109–110). It was one thing for the Occupation forces to declare the inutility of Japanese, as they were wont to do. It was totally another for a notable Japanese intellectual who made his living with his pen to concur with such an Orientalizing remark. The wholesale castigation of traditional values was about as thorough as the total praise of them during the war.

In this situation, discourse on Japan's identity of the late 1940s and the 1950s became one of comparing Japan with the West as Japan's way of convincing itself how wrong it was—a way of providing a rationale for the lost status of the wartime ideology. The West was upheld as the model and the ideal, and whatever the West had and Japan did not have was the reason for Japan's defeat and for criticizing Japan, be it its cultural traits, social institutions, or personality.

Legions of Western observers, including MacArthur (who claimed the Japanese mentality to be that of a twelve-year-old), saw and analyzed Japan against the mirror of their own social values, and in their free, unabated, naive ethnocentrism denigrated everything Japanese. Japanese intellectuals, in the postwar skeptical mood, were delighted to have their newfound conviction confirmed by observers from countries that represented a superior civilization and the new model for Japan.

Such auto-Orientalism was, as one might expect, rampant in books, magazines, and newspapers of the time. To take a few examples, in the January 1947 issue of *Chūō kōron* (Central review), one of the most popular magazines, Ishiwata Sadao, Hani Gorō, Inoue Kiyoshi, and Ishimoda Tadashi—leading scholars of the time—held a round-table discussion whose purpose was "to discuss in concrete terms backward and feudalistic elements woven into the fabric of Japanese society as reactionary factors preventing Japan's democratic revolution" (Ishiwata et al. 1947). Among these factors, Inoue suggested that Japan's unique emperor system was born because "the Meiji Restoration did not solve [the problems of] the feudal system thoroughly." Hani blamed the invasion of China and the Pacific War on the emperor system. He also spoke of "the backwardness of Japanese society."

In the March issue, Katō Hyōji (1947) blamed the failure of contemporary politics on "forces of the feudalistic bureaucracy." In the April issue, Ishiwata Sadao (1947), a member of the roundtable discussion featured in the January issue, blamed "the semi-feudalism of Japanese landlords" for the high rent for tenants. In May, Kawashima Takeyoshi (1947) argued on the "Asiatic characteristics of Japanese feudalism"; he called the adoption system, in which a person, usually a man, is adopted for the purpose of taking over the family name and the family enterprise, a form of slavery.

Tanigawa Tetsuzō, who taught at Hōsei University and was associate director of a national museum at the time of writing, criticized the Japanese national character in *Bunkaron* (1947) on several grounds. For one, in contrast to Christianity, which seeks salvation of the soul, Japanese mythology emphasizes hierarchical human relations and merely teaches obedience before authority. Second, this same mythology was responsible for the tendency of placing the interest of the nation-state above the interest of the individual. Third, the Japanese do not know how to use freedom correctly. Fourth, the Japanese do not know how to respect the individual. In short, he criticized the Japanese for not possessing values commonly accepted as Western.

Kawashima Takeyoshi, sociologist of law, was even more critical of the Japanese family institution in his *Ideorogii to shite no kazoku seido* (The family system as ideology) (1957) and *Nihon shakai no kazoku-teki kōsei* (The familistic structure of the Japanese society) (1950). In the former, he argued that Japan's defeat destroyed the power structure that had supported the old feudal ideology and removed the obstacle for the growth of a modern family morality and that this modern morality was fostered by the Occupation policy and stabilized by the new postwar constitution (Kawashima 1957:125).

This self-castigation—blaming Japan's tradition for Japan's misery—went hand in hand with the Occupation's pronouncement that virtually everything in Japan was antidemocratic and outmoded and had to be reformed. The Japanese accepted the Occupation's judgment that the West was best and Japan was its opposite. The Occupation's zeal to create a democracy from the ashes of the war and to prevent resurgence of an enemy of the Allied Powers of course did not stop at mere pronouncements. Reforms proceeded on practically all fronts of social life, from adoption of a new constitution and land reform to educational reform and dissolution of the *zaibatsu* (industrial conglomerate). As the West was represented almost solely, and mightily, by the military might of the Allied Powers, notably the United States, it was almost inevitable that the attitude of the Japanese toward the West echoed that of a hundred years before, when the Japanese were overwhelmed by Western military power and later by the glitter of Western civilization. They agreed with Western observers and were convinced that Japanese culture and social institutions were fundamentally flawed and desperately needed an overhaul. Thus, for the second time in history, Japan went through a major period of auto-Orientalism.

Ascendancy of Cultural Nationalism since the Late 1960s

It was not until the late 1960s that the balance began to tip and Japanese began to see themselves in a positive light more than in a negative light. By this time, the postwar "allergy," as this defeatist attitude of almost masochistic self-negation is sometimes called, slowly began to be outweighed by a more self-confident, self-congratulatory identity.

The end of the Allied Occupation of Japan, the signing of the peace treaty with the United States, the gradual economic recovery of the late 1950s and the 1960s all contributed to the regaining of self-confidence, or at least the lessening of the feeling of inferiority and psychological and spiritual defeat. As the postwar economy began to take off and enter the stage of rapid growth, the *Nihonjinron* too began to take a turn and to portray Japan in a more favorable light. The same social institutions and the same cultural values that had been objects of condemnation in the immediate postwar years were now seen to have positive valence: if they were not any better than those of the West, at least they were just as good. The Japanese were now finally able to take the position of a cultural relativist, rather than accepting uncritically and in toto the victor's value judgments (Aoki 1989).

Slowly regaining self-confidence, the Japanese began to marvel at the country's phenomenal economic development and to see it as a result of or at least fostered by Japan's unique social institutions, cultural values, and personality, rather than as resulting *in spite of* Japan's "pre-modern" or "feudalistic" institutions and values.

The overwhelming majority of *Nihonjinron* literature now began to discuss the unique characteristics of Japan as its strength and the basis of its global economic success. In the most recent period, the definition of Japanese cultural and national identity has been imbued even with ethnocentrism, seeing positive values in Japanese culture while denigrating the West.

The 1960s and 1970s were still decades in which negative Japan and positive Japan coexisted as uneasy bedfellows. "Critical" (or negative) *Nihonjinron* held sway early in this period, but it was slowly taken over by a more positive *Nihonjinron*. From the late 1970s on, the vast majority of *Nihonjinron* literature began to discuss the unique characteristics of Japan as its strength and as the basis of its economic success and even propounded the *Nihonjinron* thesis as Japan's prime mover.

Of late this trend has reached a hawkish zenith, where Japan is represented as a country ready to take on the West and win. Disparaging remarks by high-level politicians and officials, such as the former prime minister, Nakasone, and the former speaker of the lower house of the Diet, Sakurai, about the United States are examples.

Conclusion

In the modern history of Japan, one can identify periods of overwhelming negative self-identity and also periods of equally overwhelming positive self-identity. The first period of positive identity came in the late eighteenth century and the first half of the nineteenth century with the *kokugaku* nationalist movement. The self-confidence gained through valorization of indigenous institutions and values in this movement, however, was shattered by the overwhelming military and technological superiority of the West, forcibly thrust upon Japan through gunboat diplomacy.

Although not conquered or colonized by any Western power, Japan suffered humiliation, having to terminate its self-imposed seclusion, sign unequal trade treaties, and pay indemnities to European nations for the "wrongs" done to their citizens. As Japanese began to have more and more contact with the West—for example, by traveling to Europe and America and by having Westerners come to Japan as consultants and university professors in the guise of *oyatoi gaikokujin* (hired foreigners)—

Japanese began increasingly to see themselves as inferior in all aspects of civilization vis-à-vis the West.

Another period of negative identity came after World War II. Again Japan experienced humiliation, this time by being totally vanquished by Western military powers. The military superiority of the West, especially the United States, impressed the Japanese even more when the Allies landed on the Japanese islands and demonstrated their matériel.

In both cases, Japan reacted with almost complete denigration and self-castigation of its own culture in a process I term "auto-Orientalism." In both periods this feeling of inferiority produced adoration of the West, extending over the entire gamut of Western civilization including art and literature.

Positive self-evaluation in *Nihonjinron* has a longer and somewhat more continuous history, but it was particularly pronounced in the late Meiji and just before and during World War II, especially since alternative, negative views of Japan were all but eliminated by the forces of the state. A few people murmured comments reflecting negative valuation of Japan, but they were few indeed and they risked police repression and reprisal. A third period of positive self-evaluation is now, since the late 1960s, as Japan's economic success around the world has become more and more firmly established as a permanent order of the world. In both periods positive evaluation is all-encompassing and not limited simply to Japan's military prowess or economic power. In prewar days, Japan claimed superiority to Western civilization in spiritual power as well as in military might. Japan's unique aesthetic qualities and social institutions were not forgotten. The same may be said of *Nihonjinron* of the present time. Its contents run the gamut of the cultural catalogue from climate, creation myth, and religion to social and political values.

The contemporary period differs from the wartime situation in that there is no overt state suppression of contrary views, at least not the sort of suppression that the secret police executed during World War II. Yet the sort of negative identity that prevailed in the immediate postwar era is well nigh gone. The Japanese who are embracing the view that "Japan is number one" because of its unique qualities are doing so without obvious coercion or state promotion. Forces of suasion are more subtle and indirect. In this respect, the contemporary positive evaluation of Japan may perhaps be a stronger, more firmly rooted affair than the wartime positive evaluation. For those who believe that contemporary

Nihonjinron leads to narrow nationalism, conservatism, and rejection of a cosmopolitan outlook for the Japanese, this contemporary trend may be something to worry about.

Looking back at the vicissitudes of the varieties of Japanese self-identity from the beginning of the nineteenth century, and considering factors for its swings from positive to negative and back to positive, one can make several observations.

One is the nature of the reference group. Japan's self-identity is constructed in comparison with a civilization that is exerting predominant influence upon it. In the Tokugawa period, this referent was China. Those who sought ideological independence from China had to define Japan as non-China. In post–Meiji Restoration Japan, the referent was Europe and the United States. The definition of who the Japanese are was made in conscious comparison with the West. China was almost forgotten in this exercise.

Second, the relative strength of Japan vis-à-vis the referent is important in defining Japan in a positive or negative light. When Japan is strong militarily or economically, or at least when Japan perceives little or no threat, as was the case vis-à-vis China in the late Tokugawa period, Japan's self-definition is overwhelmingly positive.

Third, in the construction of the positive cultural identity throughout the history of modern Japan, one sees an undercurrent of nostalgic gaze to Japan's past. That is, identity is created through a concatenation of elements from the traditional past. The exercise is even narcissistic (Nosco 1990:8) in its unqualified praise of Japan for its glorious past. It arises at least in part out of dissatisfaction with the present—whether in its domestic or its international aspects—and the nostalgic, idealized construction of the past in *Nihonjinron* becomes therapeutic treatment for the malaise of the present. In this respect, the present-day *Nihonjinron* boom should be seen as part and parcel of a whole host of nostalgia movements in Japan, as seen in *furusato* (old town) revival, the popularity of *enka* (songs about once-forgotten home towns and villages), and enormous interest in the prehistory of Japan and the racial ancestry of the Japanese.

In the end, current *Nihonjinron* must be seen against the background of Japan's strong economic position worldwide. How long the positive view the Japanese have of themselves will continue will depend on Japan's geoeconomic strength relative to world economic powers, notably the United States.

References Cited

Aoki Tamotsu. 1989. *"Nihon bunkaron" no hen'yō—Sengo Nihon no bunka to aidentitii* (Transformation of *Nihonjinron*: Culture and identity in postwar Japan). Tokyo: Chūō Kōronsha.

Befu, Harumi. 1992. Symbols of nationalism and *Nihonjinron*. In *Ideology and practice in modern Japan*, ed. Roger Goodman and Kirsten Refsing, 26–46. London: Routledge.

———. 1995. Swings of Japan's identity. In *Cultural Encounters: China, Japan, and the West: Essays commemorating twenty-five years of East Asian studies at the University of Aarhus*, ed. Søren Clausen, Roy Starrs, and Anne Wedell-Wedellsborg, 241–267. Aarhus: Aarhus University Press.

Befu, Harumi; David McConnell; Sug-In Kweon; and Kazufumi Manabe. 1988. *Nihonjinron*: Whose cup of tea? *Kwansei Gakuin University Annual Studies* 37:129–133.

Dale, Peter. 1986. *The myth of Japanese uniqueness*. New York: St. Martin's.

Davis, Winston. 1976. The civil theology of Inoue Tetsujiro. *Japanese Journal of Religious Studies* 3, 1: 5–40.

Gluck, Carol. 1985. *Japan's modern myths: Ideology in the late Meiji period*. Princeton, N.J.: Princeton University Press.

Hardacre, Helen. 1989. *Shinto and the state, 1868–1988*. Princeton, N.J.: Princeton University Press.

Harootunian, Harry D. 1988. *Things seen and unseen: Discourse and ideology in Tokugawa nativism*. Chicago: University of Chicago Press.

Hasegawa Nyozekan. 1938. *Nihon-teki seikaku* (The Japanly character). Tokyo: Iwanami Shoten.

Holtom, Daniel. 1963. *Modern Japan and Shinto nationalism*. New York: Paragon.

Ikumatsu Keizō. 1963. Senzen no Nihon bunka ron (Prewar *Nihonjinron*). *Shisō*, no. 463 (January), 12–23.

Inoue Tetsujirō. 1891. *Chokugo Engi* (Commentary on the Rescript). Tokyo: Keigyōsha.

Ishiwata Sadao. 1947. Rōnō-ha riron o hihansu (Critiquing the rōnōha theory). *Chūō kōron*, April 31–45.

Ishiwata Sadao, Hani Gorō, Inoue Kiyoshi, and Ishimoda Tadashi. 1947. Minshu kakumei to Nihon no shakai (Democratic revolution and the Japanese society). *Chūō kōron*, January, 39–54.

Kamishima, Jirō. 1990. Society convergence: An alternative for the homogeneity theory. *Japan Foundation Newsletter* 17, 3: 1–6.

Kang Sang-Chōng. 1988. Nihon teki orientarizumu no genzai—Kokusai ka ni hisomu hizumi (The Japanese-style Orientalism today—Hidden traps in internationalization). *Sekai,* December, 133-139.

Katō Hyōji. 1947. Kiro ni tatsu shakaitō (The Socialist party at the crossroads). *Chūō kōron,* March, 34-39.

Kawashima Takeyoshi. 1947. Nihon hōken sei no Ajia teki seishitsu (The Asiatic character of Japanese feudalism). *Chūō kōron,* May, 6-19.

———. 1950. *Nihon shakai no kazokuteki kōsei* (The familistic structure of the Japanese society). Tokyo: Nihon Hyōron Sha.

———. 1957. *Ideorogii toshiteno kazoku seido* (The family system as ideology). Tokyo: Iwanami Shoten.

Kuki Shūzō. 1930. *"Iki" no Kōzō* (The structure of chic). Tokyo: Iwanami Shoten.

Manabe, Kazufumi, and Harumi Befu. 1989. An empirical investigation of *Nihonjinron*: The degree of exposure of Japanese to *Nihonjinron* propositions and the functions these propositions serve. *Kwansei Gakuin University Annual Studies* 38:35-62.

———. 1991. *Nihonjinron*: The discursive manifestation of cultural nationalism. *Kwansei Gakuin University Annual Studies* 40:101-115.

Miyake Setsurei. 1977 [1891]. *Shin zen bi Nihonjin* (Truth, goodness, and beauty in the Japanese) and *Gi aku ki Nihonjin* (Deception, evil, and ugliness in the Japanese). In *Nihonjinron,* ed. Ikumatsu Keizō. Tokyo: Fuzanbō.

Miller, Roy Andrew. 1982. *Japan's modern myth: The language and beyond.* New York/Tokyo: Weatherhill.

Minami Hiroshi. 1980. *Nihonjinron no keifu* (History of *Nihonjinron*). Tokyo: Kōdansha.

Minear, Richard H. 1980. Orientalism and the study of Japan. *Journal of Asian Studies* 39, 3: 507-517.

Motoyama Yukihiko. 1958. Meiji nijūnendai no seiron ni arawareta nashonarizumu (Nationalism manifested in political theories of the Meiji twenties). In *Meiji zenhanki no nashonarizumu* (Nationalism in the first half of the Meiji period), ed. Yoshio Sakata, 37-84. Tokyo: Miraisha.

Mouer, Ross E. 1983. "Orientarism" as knowledge: Lessons for Japanologists? *Keio Journal of Politics* 4:11-31.

Nishida Kitarō. 1940. *Nihon bunka no mondai* (Problems of Japanese culture). Tokyo: Iwanami Shoten.

Mouer, Ross E. 1983. "Orientarism" as knowledge: Lessons for Japanologists? *Keio Journal of Politics* 4:11–31.
Nishida Kitarō. 1940. *Nihon bunka no mondai* (Problems of Japanese culture). Tokyo: Iwanami Shoten.
Nosco, Peter. 1990. *Remembering paradise: Nativism and nostalgia in eighteenth-century Japan.* Cambridge: Harvard University Council on East Asian Studies.
Pyle, Kenneth B. 1969. *The new generation in Meiji Japan: Problems of cultural identity, 1885–1895.* Stanford, Calif.: Stanford University Press.
Said, Edward. 1978. *Orientalism.* New York: Random House.
Sakata Yoshio, ed. 1958. *Meiji zenhanki no nashonarizumu* (Nationalism in the first half of the Meiji period). Tokyo: Miraisha.
Shiga Shigetaka. 1976 [1894]. *Nihon fūkei ron* (Theory of Japanese landscape). Tokyo: Iwanami Shoten.
Shirayanagi Shūko. 1938. *Nihon minzoku to tennen* (The Japanese people and nature). Tokyo: Chikura Shobō.
Suzuki Daisetz. 1940. *Zen to Nihon bunka* (Zen and the Japanese culture). Tokyo: Iwanami Shoten.
Tanaka Yoshitau. 1924. *Kokumin dōtoku yōryō kōgi* (Lectures on the principles of national morality). Tokyo: Nihon Gakujutsu Kenkyūkai.
Tanigawa Tetsuzō. 1947. *Bunkaron* (On culture). Tokyo: Kinbundō Shuppanbu.
Uchida Roan. 1968. Rokumeikan jidai (The Rokumeikan period). In *Gendai Nihon kiroku zenshuu* (Documentary compendium on modern Japan). Vol. 4: *Bunmei kaika* (Civilization and enlightenment), ed. Shigeki Senuma, 23–31. Tokyo: Chikuma Shobō.
Watsuji Tetsurō. 1935. *Fūdo—Ningen gaku-teki kōsatsu* (The climate—Humanological considerations). Tokyo: Iwanami Shoten.

TWO

Biological Affinities of the Japanese Population

KAZURO HANIHARA

Since the middle nineteenth century, several theories have been proposed concerning the population history of the Japanese. Franz Philipp von Siebold was the first scientist to carry out anthropological studies of the Japanese. He went to Japan in 1823 as a physician of the Dutch settlement at Nagasaki and collected a large number of specimens and much information, including anthropological data, concerning Japanese culture and natural history.

Soon after the Meiji Restoration in 1868, many European and American scholars were invited by the new Japanese government to help Japan's modernization. Among them, scholars who provided important contributions to the anthropology as well as the archaeology of Japan include Edward E. Morse from Boston, Erwin von Baelz from Germany, and John Milne from England. In the late nineteenth century, Japanese students who studied abroad returned home and carried on the works initiated by these visiting scholars. Anthropology, archaeology, folklore, and related sciences have all been furthered by Japanese investigations since then.

During the last century and a half, several important theories regarding the population history of the Japanese have been proposed on the basis of evidence unearthed through osteology, somatology, genetics, dental anthropology, and so forth. Most of these theories have had to be revised or abandoned in the light of newer findings. In addition, important findings pointed out by earlier scholars that were sometimes ignored by later investigators should be reevaluated in the light of recent evidence and methodology.

Representative theories regarding the population history of the Japanese so far proposed may be grouped into five categories: (1) replacement theory argued by Morse (1879), Koganei (1893), and others; (2) dual physique theory by Baelz (1883, 1885); (3) hybridization theory by argued Kiyono (1949) and Kohama (1960); (4) transformation theory argued by Hasebe (1940) and Suzuki (1969); and (5) migration theory argued by Kanaseki (1976) and his successors.

The replacement theory emphasizes that the Neolithic Jōmon population—Jōmonese—was replaced by other population who gave rise to modern Japanese. The dual physique theory stresses somatological heterogeneity in recent Japanese. The hybridization theory states that the Jōmonese who intermixed with the North Asians gave rise to the present-day Ainu, and those intermixed with South Asians to form modern non-Ainu Japanese. The transformation theory attributes special importance to gradual changes in morphology that took place during the course of microevolution, stressing a direct lineage from the Jōmonese to modern Japanese.

These theories cannot explain, however, all the available evidence related to the Japanese population. In particular, issues that remain unexplained include geographic variations in modern Japanese; genetic as well as morphological clines in the Japanese archipelago; close affinities among the Ainu, Ryūkyūans (from Okinawa island), and Jōmonese; the large extent of Northeast Asian influence on Japanese; and regional differences in various kinds of cultural elements.

The migration theory, which assumes a fairly large scale of migration from Northeast Asia in the Aeneolithic Yayoi age, seems to cover a number of weaknesses in the previous theories. According to Kanaseki's original view (Kanaseki, Nagai, and Sano, 1960), however, the scale of migration was so small that the indigenous Japanese people were influenced little by the migrants. Nevertheless, a number of later findings have unveiled the large effect of the migrants on the Japanese as a whole.

During the last thirty years I have collected dental and cranial data from different local groups of the Japanese and analyzed them using several methods of numerical taxonomy. The most basic important results obtained so far are as follows:

1. Suzuki (1982) pointed out that the Upper Palaeolithic Minatogawa humans from Okinawa Island were morphologically much closer to the Liujiang humans from South China than to the Upper

Cave humans in North China. Suzuki also emphasized the close similarity between the Minatogawa humans and the Jōmonese. A principal component analysis (PCA) of cranial measurements confirms Suzuki's view, suggesting further that the Jōmonese are close to the Upper Palaeolithic southeast Asians in cranial morphology (K. Hanihara 1984).

2. In the early Yayoi age, populations that were largely different in skeletal morphology from indigenous people, or the descendants of the Jōmonese, appeared abruptly in northern Kyūshū. Kanaseki and his colleagues (1960) emphasized that they were migrants, probably from the northern part of the Korean peninsula. The number of sites that yielded migrant-type skeletal remains has increased during the last thirty years, and morphological as well as cultural differences between the so-called migrants and indigenous populations became more evident. Statistical analyses of cranial data from the two groups of Yayoi populations and those from different populations on the Asian mainland show close affinities between the migrants and the Northeast Asians in East Siberia, the northeastern part of China, and Mongolia. It is quite likely, therefore, that the Yayoi migrants originated in Northeast Asia (K. Hanihara, 1984).

3. A PCA of cranial measurements from the Japanese population of different ages and regions show a difference between the Jōmonese and later populations. The Jōmonese form a single group with relatively small variation; the populations of the Yayoi, protohistoric Kofun, and recent ages show much wider ranges of variability and a trend toward bipolarization, one pole of which corresponds to the lineage of migrants and the other to that of the Jōmonese. At the same time, the former tends to be distributed in western Japan and the latter in eastern Japan. This trend may suggest that one part of the Japanese, particularly those in western Japan, has been largely influenced by migrants in and after the Yayoi age. It is also noteworthy that the difference between the two groups is particularly evident between northern Kyūshū and the other regions in the Yayoi age (third century B.C.–A.D. third century), between western and eastern Japan in the protohistoric Kofun age (A.D. fourth–sixth centuries), and between the Honshū-Kyūshū-Shikoku and Hokkaidō (Ainu)-Okinawa (Ryūkyū) areas in the recent age. Such a chronological change in regional difference suggests that the influence of the migrants extended gradually to eastern Japan (K. Hanihara 1987b).

4. Geographic variations in recent Japanese provide another important basis for reconstructing the population history. For example, the distribution pattern of the ABO blood group genes, individual stature, cephalic indices, and so forth shows an evident cline from western to eastern Japan. Cephalic indices and cranial measurements in recent Japanese also show geographic variations and tend to become closer to Ainu as one goes northeastward along Honshū. People are also taller in western Japan, particularly in the northern Kyūshū, Chūgoku, and Kinki districts. Interestingly, all the characteristics of the western Japanese are closer to the Northeast Asian populations, and those of the eastern Japanese, to the Jōmonese and Ainu (K. Hanihara 1985).

5. Ainu, who were once considered a branch of the Caucasians, and Ryūkyūans resemble each other not only in morphology but also in the distribution pattern of different genes. Statistical analyses of cranial measurements further show that the Jōmonese are much closer to these two populations than to recent Japanese on the main islands—Honshū, Kyūshū, and Shikoku. This fact seems to suggest that the Ainu and Ryūkyūans are influenced little or not at all by the migrants from Northeast Asia. Basically the same idea is also provided through studies on nonmetric cranial traits (Ossenberg 1986, Dodo and Ishida 1988). Historically, Ainu and Ryūkyūans were almost independent of Japan's imperial court or feudal government until recent times. Such a political, and probably geographical, isolation may have been responsible for their retaining their own gene pool (K. Hanihara 1984, 1990).

6. Geographically isolated groups in Japan are more or less similar to the Ainu, Ryūkyūans, and Jōmonese in dental morphology, but different from a majority of the modern Japanese (T. Hanihara 1989a, 1989b). At the same time, a close similarity between the Jōmonese-Ainu-Ryūkyū group and the Philippine Negritos in dental characteristics is recognized (T. Hanihara 1989b, T. Hanihara and K. Hanihara 1990). Taking these findings together with Omoto's (1984, 1986) genetic studies on Negritos into consideration, we can postulate that the Jōmonese characteristics still maintained in some of the modern Japanese may have been derived originally from the early Southeast Asians.

7. A computer simulation based on the annual rates of population increase and secular changes in cranial morphology estimates the total number of migrants from the Asian mainland at 400,000 to more than 1,000,000 during the thousand years from the beginning of the Yayoi age to the eighth century (K. Hanihara 1987a).

Although the range of estimates is wide and the initial values used in simulation are not reliable enough, the estimates seem to be not far from fact because morphological characteristics and gene combinations in the modern Japanese show dominant Northeast Asian elements. It is probable, therefore, that a fairly large number of people migrated to the Japanese archipelago, despite the view of most earlier anthropologists and archaeologists that the number of migrants was almost negligible.

8. Heterogeneity in the Japanese population was proved on the basis of dental morphology. Similarity between the Ainu and Ryūkyūans and differences between these two groups and the Japanese main islanders were first reported by me and others using dental characteristics (K. Hanihara, Masuda, and Tanaka 1974). Turner and his colleagues (Turner 1976, 1986, 1987; Turner and Hanihara 1977) as well as Brace and his colleagues (Brace and Nagai 1982; Brace, Brace, and Leonard 1989), who conducted dental anthropological studies on the Japanese and surrounding populations, recognize apparent differences among the Ainu-Jōmonese and modern main island groups. The former is represented by "sundadont" and the latter by "sinodont" dental patterns in Turner's terminology.

9. Nonhuman evidence almost exactly parallels human geographic variation in the Japanese archipelago, as, for example, one observes that northeastern Japanese dogs are similar to those of Southeast Asia, and western Japanese dogs are similarly comparable to North Asian dogs in genetic polymorphisms. Moriwaki and colleagues (see Yonekawa et al. 1988) found almost the same trends in the distribution pattern of Japanese mice, *Mus musculus molossinus*. In other words, dogs and mice similar to those in Southeast Asia are distributed in the areas where the Jōmonese characteristics are still retained. Dogs and mice in northeastern Japan, therefore, probably were introduced from Southeast Asia in or earlier than the Jōmon age, and those in western Japan from North Asia in or later than the Yayoi age.

Putting all these finding together, we postulate (1) that the Jōmon tradition is still retained in at least part of Japan's local areas; (2) that the geographic variation in physical characteristics does not show a random distribution but rather reveals clines running through the Japanese archipelago from northeast to southwest; (3) that close affinities between the Northeast Asians and Japanese have become evident after the Yayoi age; (4) that the Jōmonese, present-day Ainu, and Ryūkyūans closely resemble each other but differ significantly from a majority of modern Japanese in the main islands; and (5) that cultural elements are not uniform throughout eastern and western Japan. In sum, the Japanese population consists of at least two elements, one of which came from Southeast Asia and the other from Northeast Asia. The same is also true in cultural evidence.

Another point of importance is that the difference between the two elements has become evident since the Yayoi age and is still retained in the modern Japanese. On the basis of this evidence, we may employ a "dual structure model" for the population history of the Japanese as a working hypothesis. I would like to emphasize that this model can be applied not only to physical traits but also to certain culture evidence in Japan.

Figure 1 is a schematic figure drawn on the basis of the first and second principal components that were computed from nine representative cranial measurements. Viewed from the perspective of the dual structure model, this figure may be interpreted as follows: The palaeolithic Southeast Asians probably gave rise to the Jōmonese on one hand, to the Neolithic Northeast Asians on the other. The former changed to the present-day Ainu and Ryūkyūans in the course of microevolution, the latter to the modern Northeast Asians, who adapted to the extremely cold climate.

In and after the Yayoi age, migrants who settled in the Japanese archipelago admixed with indigenous people who were the descendants of the Jōmonese. As a result of this admixture—which took place in different magnitudes in different regions—the Japanese main islanders as a whole experienced different secular changes from those experienced by the Ainu-Ryūkyūan group. Although this hypothesis should be refined as physical as well as cultural evidence is accumulated, it seems to be useful in understanding the history of the Japanese population and culture.

Figure 1

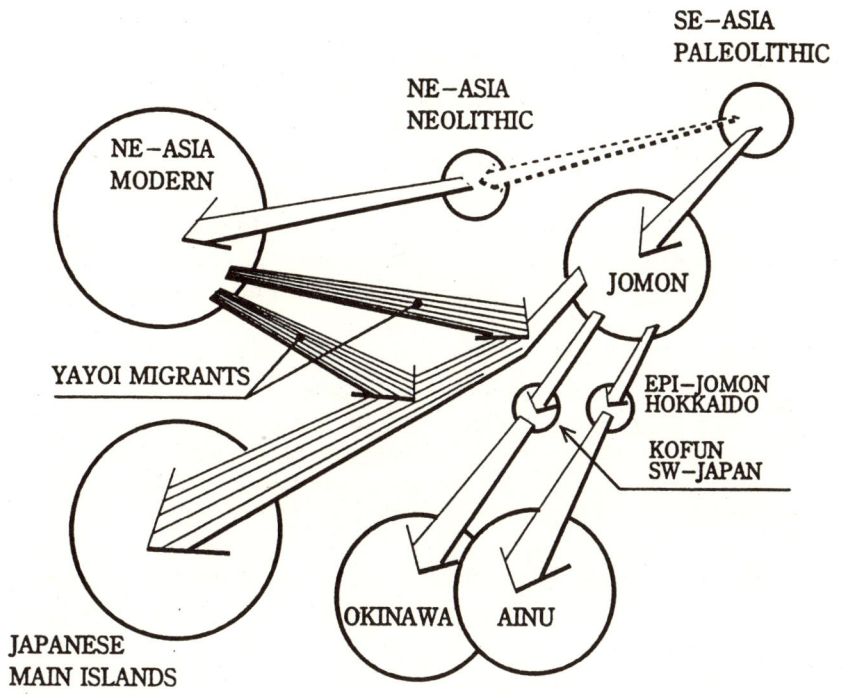

Drawn from the first and second principal component scores based on nine male cranial measurements.

References

von Baelz, E. 1883, 1885. Die korperliche Eigenschaften der Japaner. *Mitt. Deutsch. Ges. Natur u. Volkerk. Ostasiens* 28:330–359, 32:35–103.

Brace, C. L., and M. Nagai. 1982. Japanese tooth size, past and present. *Am. J. Phys. Anthrop.* 59:399–411.

Brace, C. L.; M. Brace; and W. R. Leonard. 1989. Reflections on the face of Japan: A multivariate craniofacial and odontometric perspective. *Am. J. Phys. Anthrop.* 78:93–113.

Dodo, Y., and H. Ishida. 1988. Nonmetric analyses of the Doigahama crania of the Aeneolithic Yayoi period in western Japan. In *The genesis of the Japanese population and culture*, ed. Dept. Anat., Kyūshū Univ., pp. 127–142. Tokyo: Rokko Shuppan. In Japanese with English summary.

Hanihara, K. 1984. Origins and affinities of Japanese viewed from cranial measurements. *Acta Anthropogenetica* 8:149–158.

———. 1985. Geographic variation of modern Japanese and its relationship to the origin of Japanese. *Homo* 36:1–10.

———. 1987a. Estimation of the number of early migrants to Japan: A simulative study. *J. Anthrop. Soc. Nippon* 95:391–403.

———. 1987b. Anthropological aspects of the Pacific and Japan Sea coasts, with special reference to formation of the Japanese population. *Jinrui kagaku* (union of nine academic societies in human sciences), 1–13, 137–140. In Japanese with English summary.

———. 1990. Emishi, Ezo, and Ainu: An anthropological perspective. *Japan Review* 1:35–48.

———. 1991. Dual structure model for the population history of the Japanese. *Japan Review*, no. 2, pp. 1–33.

Hanihara, K., and T. Hanihara. 1990. Comparative studies on dentition from Oceania and pan-Pacific populations. *J. Anthrop. Soc. Nippon* 98:187.

Hanihara, K.; T. Masuda; and T. Tanaka. 1974. Affinities of dual characteristics in the Okinawa Islanders. *J. Anthrop. Soc. Nippon* 82:75–82.

Hanihara, T. 1989a. Comparative studies of dental characteristics in the Aogashima islanders. *J. Anthrop. Soc. Nippon* 97:9–22.

———. 1989b. Comparative studies of geographically isolated populations in Japan based on dental measurements. *J. Anthrop. Soc. Nippon* 97:95–107.

Hasebe, K. 1940. Taiko no Nihon-jin (The ancient Japanese). *J. Anthrop. Soc. Nippon* 55:27–34.

Kanaseki, T. 1976. *Nihon-minzoku no kigen* (The origin of the Japanese). Tokyo: Hōsei Univ. Press.

Kanaseki, T.; M. Nagai; and H. Sano. 1960. Craniological studies of the Yayoi-period ancients, excavated at the Doigahama site, Yamaguchi Prefecture. *Jinruigaku kenkyū* 7 (suppl.): 1–36. In Japanese with English summary.

Kiyono, K. 1949. *Kodai jinkotsu no kenkyū ni motozuku Nihon jinshu-ron* (The origin of Japanese as viewed from skeletal remains). Tokyo: Iwanami Shoten.

Koganei, Y. 1893. Beitrage zur physischen Anthropologic der Aino. I: Untersuchungen am Skelett. *Mitteil. med. Fak. Kaiser.* (Univ. Tokyo) 2:1–149.

Kohama, M. 1960. Seitai-keisokugaku-teki ni mita Nihon-jin no kosei to kigen ni kansuru kōsatsu (An anthropological study of the Japanese: On the local difference and the origin of the Japanese). *Quart. J. Anthrop.* 7:56–65.

Milne, J. 1882. Note on the Koro-pokguru or pit dwellers of Yezo and the Kurile Islands. *Trans. Asiat. Soc. Japan* 10:187–198.

Morse, E. S. 1879. *Shell mounds of Omori.* Vol. 1, pt. 1. Tokyo: Mem. Sci. Dept., Univ. Tokyo.

Omoto, K. 1984. The Negritos: Genetic origins and microevolution. *Acta Anthropogenetica* 8:137–147.

———. 1986. Higashi Asia-jin no Kiso-Shudan (Racial formation in East Asia and the Pacific). In *Nihon-jin no kigen* (The origin of the Japanese), ed. K. Hanihara, 139–160. Tokyo: Shogakukan.

Ossenberg, N. S. 1986. Isolate conservatism and hybridization in the population history of Japan: The evidence of nonmetric cranial traits. In *Prehistoric hunter-gatherers in Japan*, ed. T. Akazawa and C. M. Aikens, 190–215. Tokyo: Univ. Tokyo Press.

Suzuki, H. 1969. Microevolutionary changes in Japanese population from the prehistoric age to the present day. *J. Fac. Sci. Univ. Tokyo*, sec. 5, 3:279–308.

———. 1982. Skulls of the Minatogawa man. In *The Minatogawa man: The Upper Pleistocene man from the island of Okinawa*, ed. H. Suzuki and K. Hanihara, 7–49. Univ. Tokyo, Univ. Mus. Bull., no. 19.

Turner, C. G., II. 1976. Dental evidence on the origins of the Ainu and Japanese. *Science* 193: 911–913.

———. 1986. Dentochronological separation estimates for Pacific rim populations. *Science* 232:1140–1142.

———. 1987. Late Pleistocene and holocene population history of East Asia based on dental variation. *Am. J. Phys. Anthrop.* 73:305–321.

Turner, C. G, II, and K. Hanihara. 1977. Additional features of Ainu dentition. *Am. J. Phys. Anthrop.* 46:13–24.

Yonekawa, H.; K. Moriwaki; O. Gotoh; N. Miyashita; Y. Matsushima; L. Shi; W. S. Cho; X. L. Zhen; and Y. Tagashira. 1988. Hybrid origin of Japanese mice *Mus musculus molossinus:* Evidence from restriction analysis of mitochondrial DNA. *Mol. Biol. Evol.* 5:63–78.

THREE

Connected Visions of Female Identity: Autobiographical Writings by Tamura Toshiko and Miyamoto Yuriko

REIKO YONOGI

"Identity" is an important concept for much of modern cultural and literary criticism, and both self-discovery and the search for identity have become main themes in literature not only in the West but also in Japan. An American feminist literary critic, Elaine Showalter (1977, 13), has identified "self-discovery," "a search for identity," as the main theme of women's literature since 1920. During the early decades of the twentieth century, many women began to be published in Japan. Many wrote about the situation of women from a feminist perspective, and their concerns naturally centered on female identity. Among Japanese female writers who were especially concerned with women's rights and women's position in society were Tamura Toshiko (1884–1945) and Miyamoto Yuriko (1899–1951). Their novels and short stories dramatize female characters' search for identity in modern society, and their works are united by a feminist consciousness. Although both writers rely upon an autobiographical mode and both are concerned with women's freedom and autonomy, Tamura Toshiko is more of the aesthetic school and Miyamoto Yuriko is more socially oriented.

This essay examines three autobiographical works: Tamura's "Onna sakusha" (A woman writer, 1913) and *Miira no kuchibeni* (Painted lips of a mummy, 1913) and Miyamoto's *Nobuko* (1926). Although none of these works is autobiography per se, all are considered autobiographical by common consent. Tanaka Yukiko says in her introduction to the collection of fiction *To Live and to*

Japanese names are given in the traditional order, surnames first.

Write (1987, xi), "The autobiographical form has indeed been the most basic and persisting approach to Japanese fiction writing since the turn of the century." Both writers emphatically identify with their main female characters and write the characters' stories as part of their own continuing process of defining a female identity. Thus, as critic Judith Kegan Gardiner says (1981, 361), "Female identity is a process and writing by women engages us in this process as the female self seeks to define itself in the experience of creating art."

Rita Felski, in her book *Beyond Feminist Aesthetics: Feminist Literature and Social Change* (1989, 133), talking about a schematic overview of Western female narrative, says that "the eighteenth-century novel is unable to conceive of conscious rebellion on the part of the heroine, and the nineteenth-century novel traces an inward awakening and resistance which is, however, crushed by an intransigent social order"; she notes that the genre most clearly identified with contemporary feminist writing is the narrative of female self-discovery, which tells "a story of resistance and survival made possible by the mediation of the women's movement, which provides an ideological framework sanctioning the self-conscious affirmation of a gendered identity." Although Felski (1989, chap. 3) is not talking specifically about autobiographical writing, her insight can be extended to include female autobiographical narrative or fiction insofar as the distinction between autobiography and fiction has recently become blurred. Talking about women's narrative strategies, Nancy Walker in her *Feminist Alternatives* (1990, 77) says that "a blurring of the distinctions between genres, particularly between fiction and autobiography is due to less fixed, more fluid concepts of identity for women," citing Gardiner's contention that female identity is a process and primary identity for women is more flexible and relational than for men. Gardiner herself says (1981, 355) that "women's novels are often called autobiographical and women's autobiographies novelistic.... Because of the continual crossing of self and other, women's writing may blur the public and private."

During the Meiji period (1868–1912) in Japan, a great number of Western philosophical and literary works were introduced into Japan and translated. John Stuart Mill's *The Subjection of Women* (1869), translated in 1879, influenced Japanese feminism. In drama, Ibsen was especially popular. *A Doll's House* (1879) was translated and published in January 1910; first performed in the fall of 1911, it became a sensation. As part of this adaptation of foreign culture, Western cultural values as well as styles became influential. In September 1911, Hiratsuka Raicho (1886–1971) and several other women formed Seito, which Hiratsuka led.[1] Raicho insisted that every woman had to awaken as an individual human being and liberate herself from the obstacles to her development, had to become a fulfilled person before being a wife or mother. Seito started a journal under the same name; it was designed to encourage "creative freedom and the development of women's genius." Thus the group became a symbol of Japan's new liberated woman, and the appellation "New Woman" was first applied to these Seito women. Although the journal lasted less than five years, it contributed to the later feminist movement. Thus, during the early decades of the twentieth century, new types of women appeared both in real life and in literary works.

Tamura Toshiko was born in 1884 (Meiji 17) in an old downtown section of Tokyo. At the age of eighteen, she became a pupil of Koda Rohan, a famous male writer, and hoped to become a writer herself. There she met Tamura Shogyo, also a protégé of Rohan's. They fell in love but did not marry because he was going to the United States to study. Seven years later when Shogyo finally returned, they did marry, but even early in their marriage they often found themselves in conflict. The arguments and quarrels from this period of their lives are described in several of Tamura's works. Although her personal life was not so peaceful, the period when she was married to Shogyo (they separated in 1916) was the most productive and fruitful time of her professional development as a writer. It was almost as if their conflict and battle gave her enormous energy and material to write about. In 1918, Toshiko followed Suzuki Etsu, a journalist and her lover of a few years, to Vancouver, Canada, where she stayed for the next eighteen years. In 1936, she returned to Japan, but her creative ability was dwindling by then, and she could hardly make ends meet. In December 1938, when she was fifty-four, Toshiko went to China as a reporter for a Japanese book publisher. She stayed in China and in Shanghai began *Women's Voice*, a magazine for Chinese women. Tamura Toshiko died of a stroke in April 1945. Her life had been as turbulent as her heroines' lives.

Tamura Toshiko wrote in a period when feminist consciousness was just beginning to appear in Japan. She contributed a short

---

[1] Seito is the literal translation of the Bluestocking society, women's literary clubs of eighteenth-century England.

story, "Ikichi" (Live blood) to the first issue of *Seito*, although she was not a core member of the group. Several other female writers appeared about this time, and their works reflected the desires of the newly awakened woman who asserted herself and longed for freedom and autonomy. Among them, Tamura Toshiko was a pioneer. She is regarded as the first Japanese woman to write frankly about women's internal struggles and about the real battles and conflicts between men and women from a female perspective (Senuma 1990, 212). In her autobiographical works, she repeatedly described the conflict between husband and wife based on her relationship with her husband.

"A Woman Writer" deals with a troubled relationship between a female author (who represents Toshiko herself) and her husband and with the fictional author's difficulties as a writer. The character knows that her relationship with her husband is not satisfactory, but she cannot break it off: "The woman writer had in fact considered living alone more than once; she'd been tormented by the idea. But she knew she couldn't do this. It wasn't possible to go back to the life of living alone" (Tamura 1987, 1:303; Tanaka 1987, 16). Here is Toshiko's recurring theme of conflict between desire for autonomy and desire for companionship. We see here her female self defined in terms of a relationship; she is unable to break the connection and to assert an autonomous identity.

The cost of that connection is expressed through the symbol of face powder, which is almost a leitmotif in many of Tamura's works: The protagonist, who is the author's persona in this work, always wears makeup. She hides her natural self with powder and is emotionally uncomfortable unless she puts on makeup. She feels creative when she is in front of the mirror. Her writing is full of the smell of powder.

> The woman writer used powder all the time. Even though she was about to reach thirty, she wore heavy makeup. When no one was around, she made up her face like a stage actress and secretly enjoyed looking at herself in the mirror. She could not do without face powder, and in fact even wore it when she was in bed, as long as she didn't feel too ill. When she had no powder on her face, she felt as if she were dragging around something ugly and bare on her body. When she didn't wear face powder, her emotions became jagged...[and] her mood deteriorated; she became sulky and lost all desire to be flirtatious. She feared this state more than anything else. And that was why she had to cover her naked face with powder all the time. (Tamura 1987, 1:296–97; Tanaka 1987, 12)

In putting on makeup one hides one's real self and identity behind a mask, transforms oneself into something different, shows others a false self. Ogata Akiko (1984, 141–42) criticizes this "face powder" aspect of Toshiko's work: "If it does not gaze at a natural face, real literature won't grow. In the disguise of makeup, a woman is content with being female and does not try to breathe beyond."[2] If women put on makeup only for men, their desire for approval itself contradicts the desire to be equal with men as individuals.

A woman may also, however, wear makeup for the sheer joy of artistic expression for herself and the creation of beauty without reference to another audience:

> The woman writer did not forget to make up her face even on days when she had a great deal of difficulty with the writing she had promised to do. She knew that as she prepared the powder in front of the mirror, ideas often came to her. When she touched the tip of her finger to the powder melted in the water, the cold sensation seemed to release a refreshing image in her mind, and as she went on brushing the powder on her face, the idea slowly developed. This had happened more than times. Most of her writing, therefore, had been born out of face powder, and so it had the smell of powder. (Tamura 1987, 1:297; Tanaka 1987, 12–13)

Makeup can thus be a source of creative energy as well as a mask. It is also possible that the woman writer, writing in a time when only limited images of women were available, needed makeup to preserve integrity rather than confront male power directly with a naked face, without any protection.

In *Painted Lips of a Mummy*, Tamura expands some of the themes she treated in her previous works. The story is based on the author's own experience about the time she was writing *Akirame* (Resignation) in 1910. This is again the story of a marital conflict of a writer couple based on her own experience. The female protagonist is named Minoru, an unusual name for a woman. Tamura has given her female character a unisex (but usually male) name, apt for a female character trying to make it on her own and find her own identity. The couple, both struggling writers, are unhappy because they are poor and their works do not sell. Suffering from inadequacy and depression, they hurt each other. One day Yoshio, the husband, brings home an

---

[2] Although most of Tamura's writings are known to be autobiographical, Ogata here seems to superpose the writer Tamura on her fictional persona.

advertisement of a literary award. Aware that his own creativity is declining and that he cannot produce literary work of merit, he urges his wife to enter the competition. Minoru is unwilling and resents Yoshio's forcing her to write for money. Yet her feminine self feels compassion for Yoshio, and she persuades herself that if writing a story makes him happy, she will do it. Under his pressure, Minoru finally finishes the manuscript on the deadline date and sends it in. She is not satisfied with the work, but to their surprise, it wins the competition. Yoshio tells her, "You ought to be thankful to me because I forced you to write it," and she agrees. The award money temporarily saves their degenerating marriage.

Despite some setbacks, Minoru gradually develops a strong sense of individual self and confidence after she wins the literary award. As time goes on, however, Minoru realizes that she cannot be satisfied with the result of the competition and that she has to work even harder.

> Since then Minoru had begun working with more specific purpose. Her eyes which had been prone to be closed until then were clearly opening. At the same time, Yoshio became more and more distant. Often she ignored him. Often she did not pay attention to whatever he said. What controlled her was no longer Yoshio. For the first time in her life, what controlled her was herself. The haughtiness that Yoshio often had hated in Minoru now came to be hidden where Yoshio could not see. And in that hidden place, Minoru's pride grew stronger. (Tamura, 1962, 494–95; translation mine)

Yet for all her strong individuality and desire for independence and autonomy, Minoru still needs the Other from whom she longs to receive emotional support and consolation. At the end of the story, the relationship between Minoru and Yoshio is ambiguous: Minoru, who has found her own way and desire, is nonetheless physically unable to break away from her husband, who has lost his self-confidence. One night Minoru has a strange dream in which she is looking at a male mummy and a female mummy in a big glass case. They look gray. The male mummy lies on top of the female mummy, whose lips are painted bright red. Here we find again Tamura's theme of masking and makeup: even a woman's dead body needs makeup. Minoru finds the dream interesting and believes that it must be an intimation of some kind, but Yoshio does not pay attention and scorns the idea, saying that he doesn't like to talk about a "dream." The scene indicates a great gap opening between a man who doesn't want to talk about a "dream" and a woman who finds her dream appealing and regards it as a gateway to personal transformation. Since a dream can often be a source of inspiration, Yoshio's refusal to take Minoru's dream seriously shows his dismissal of her artistic vision. At the same time, his rejection of her dream indicates his unconscious rejection of their relationship. Minoru realizes that their relationship is like that of mummies in a case: dead and confined. Yet the image of a "female mummy whose face looks like a wooden doll with big eyes and bright red lips" is strikingly vivid. These mummies, which appear to be making love, symbolize Minoru's desire for physical intimacy even in the absence of spiritual rapport. Thus, Minoru's defiance of male authority, her desire for autonomy, and her own identity are all interwoven with her desire for intimacy and relationship. Tamura's work, here as elsewhere, remains fundamentally concerned with the personal, the individual.

In contrast to Tamura's works, which mirror the frustrations of the women of her time in their private worlds, Miyamoto Yuriko, a writer of the next generation, developed her literary world by facing her time directly, integrating women's concerns with the growing social movements of her time. Like Tamura's works, however, many of Miyamoto's works are highly autobiographical, including *Nobuko*.

At the age of nineteen, Miyamoto accompanied her father, an architect, on a business trip to New York, where she enrolled at Columbia University as an auditor. There she met a Japanese student of the Persian language, Araki Shigeru, who was fifteen years older, and married him against her parents' wishes. The marriage proved to be a failure.

Nobuko deals with Miyamoto's experience in New York and her marriage with Araki. The novel, completed in 1926 when she was twenty-seven and written at the early stage of her literary career, is considered to be her masterpiece, and it is no doubt the best known and most widely read among her works. It tells the story of the self-development of a progressive young woman who is an aspiring writer. She accompanied her father to New York so she would have the chance to live as she wanted. She felt the environment in Japan too confining and wanted to cast away a life like that of "a plant in a greenhouse." The novel covers a period of seven years from Nobuko's (Miyamoto's) initial encounter with Tsukuda (Araki). It follows their marriage in New York, their life back in Tokyo, and their final breakup.

The novel is not only about a personal failed marriage but also about the patriarchal social and family system surrounding and constructing it. Although Nobuko has vague doubts about the idea of marriage, she also has an idealistic view of marriage in which both man and woman can grow together and elevate each other. Thus, she actually proposes to Tsukuda, saying (Miyamoto 1962, 140–42; translations mine), "If I marry, I want nobody but you." Tsukuda, who does not think he can bring up the subject of marriage because of his lower social standing, is overwhelmed by joy. Nobuko continues, "I love you but I love my work also, and I can't give up my work, although I may not produce great work of art." Tsukuda responds, "You never need to worry about that. I want to make you accomplish your aspiration even if I give up myself. I am not looking for a housewife." Tsukuda also sympathizes with Nobuko's preference not to have children, and thus Tsukuda emerges, even by today's standard, as a progressive man of great understanding.

As soon as they are married, however, Nobuko feels increasingly confined by married life. She finds Tsukuda unmotivated, ordinary, and complacent. Although Tsukuda tells Nobuko that he does not expect her to be a common domestic wife, she finds herself trapped in that role. She says (Miyamoto 1962, 268), "When a man marries, he is still a man as he used to be, but a woman seems to be expected to acquire special wifely qualities. It is frightening to think that the 'self' is going to disappear." Nobuko, who had greater privilege than most other women of her time, is frustrated that she now has to feel grateful to her husband for things she took for granted before becoming a wife.

> At least in most people's eyes it wasn't he who had taken undue advantage. She had gone on trips by herself, she had stayed in bed late in the morning. And yet, she couldn't help feeling annoyed at the notion that those small freedoms were granted to her because she was his legitimate wife. It was disheartening to see her husband assume she was content on the basis of these insignificant freedoms. (Miyamoto 1962, 278; Tanaka 1987, 61)

After much psychological struggle and self-searching, Nobuko declares her desire for a divorce. In the last pages of the novel, she tells herself never to become a domesticated bird.

Nobuko's decision is supported by her female friend Motoko (based upon the character of Yuasa Yoshiko), a scholar of Russian literature, whom Nobuko meets during her deteriorating marriage. The two women become good friends. In her second book of the trilogy, Miyamoto develops Nobuko's relationship with Motoko

(Yuasa), with whom Nobuko (Miyamoto) lives for the next several years.

In breaking away from Tsukuda and patriarchal authority, Nobuko tries to find her own female identity. She achieves this status with the support of her female friend Motoko, who provides a mirror in which Nobuko's own female identity is reflected. As Felski (1989, 131) says, "Some form of at least temporary separation from traditional heterosexual relations deeply ingrained with patterns of subordination and domination is a necessary precondition for any gains in self-knowledge." In her real life after the divorce from Araki, Miyamoto's relationship with Yuasa Yoshiko became an increasingly important element in the formation of her career as a feminist writer. In 1927, Yuasa Yoshiko invited Miyamoto to join her on a visit to Russia, which was the life-long dream of this scholar of Russian literature. Their memorable trip lasted two and a half years, and Miyamoto came back from the journey a Marxist. As a Communist party member, she was imprisoned off and on from the early 1930s until the end of World War II. Her second husband, Miyamoto Kenji, was imprisoned for twelve years. After the war, she wrote prolifically, mostly in the autobiographical mode, until her death in 1951.

Carol Gilligan in *In a Different Voice* (1982, 7) writes that for women, "identity is defined in a context of relationship" and quotes Nancy Chodorow that "in any given society, feminine personality comes to define itself in relation and connection to other people more than masculine personality does." Mary Mason in her introduction to *Journeys: Autobiographical Writings by Women* (Mason and Green 1979, xiii) says that "in women's autobiographical writing, the self-portrait often includes the real presence and recognition of another consciousness." Susan Stanford Friedman in her essay "Woman's Autobiographical Selves" (1988, 41) also cites Chodorow: "Masculine personality comes to be defined more in terms of denial of relation and connection, whereas feminine personality comes to include a fundamental definition of self in relationship." Although these ideas come from Western critics, I would argue that the ideas they present apply to Japanese as well as Western women. Chodorow's psychological paradigm, like many psychological paradigms, can transcend cultural borders as long as its premises hold. Her premise is that because women care for very small children, males can differentiate themselves from their mothers early whereas females continue to identify with their mothers. In short, these critics say that women tend to define themselves in relation to an Other, whether that Other be a man, a woman, God, or the community. This concept of women's relational identity is substantiated in both Tamura's and Miyamoto's female characters, although the degree and quality of relational identity is different in the works of the two women.

Tamura's female characters, although they struggle for autonomy and identity, stay more or less in the traditional framework. Her female characters' desire for their own identity and independence is interwoven with desire for connection and relationship. Thus, their vision of identity comprises both subjectivity and connection. In her *Fujin to bungaku* (Women and literature, 1948) Miyamoto (1980, 12:306) criticized Tamura for treating male-female relationships in a small private world and not in a larger social context, but she also acknowledged that Japanese society at that time was not yet receptive to radical ideas. Miyamoto's character, Nobuko, finally breaks away from Tsukuda and achieves identity with the support of her female friend Motoko. In her later works, Miyamoto's viewpoint expands to include a larger society, and she defines herself in social and historical frameworks. In both cases, the quest for a new female identity began when the women's existence under patriarchy became stifling and when they experienced "emptiness" and "frustration" in their daily lives. As Carol Christ (1980, 13) says, "Women's spiritual quest begins in an experience of nothingness and then awakening follows."

Inasmuch as individual identity is always linked to the social world, talking about identity is talking about the Self-Other relationship and is thus relational for both men and women. However, as Chodorow and Gardiner contend and as both Tamura's and Miyamoto's female characters substantiate, women define themselves more in terms of relationships with others than men do. Thus, although both writers define selfhood in relationship to others, the differences in the definition of the Other in their works rest upon the expanding social concerns of twentieth-century Japanese women. Writing in an earlier milieu, Tamura confines her vision to specific male-female relationships, and her symbolic representation of self-presentation remains preoccupied with images of makeup; Miyamoto is able to broaden her use of the autobiographical mode to encompass such imagery as the caged bird, which reflects her desire that society should be changed. By placing her character in a concrete historical and social framework,

Miyamoto made her character universal. Either way, the writers' connections to the Other clearly empowered their creative identities.

References

Akiko Ogata. 1984. *Sakuhin no naka no onnatachi: Meiji Taisho bungaku o yomu.* Tokyo: Domesu Shuppan.
Christ, Carol. 1980. *Diving deep and surfacing: Women writers on spiritual quest.* Boston: Beacon Press.
Felski, Rita. 1989. *Beyond feminist aesthetics: Feminist literature and social change.* Cambridge: Harvard University Press.
Friedman, Susan Stanford. 1988. Women's autobiographical selves: Theory and practice. In *The private self: Theory and practice of women's autobiographical writings,* ed. Shari Benstock. Chapel Hill: University of North Caroline Press.
Gardiner, Judith Kegan. 1981. On female identity and writing by women. *Critical Inquiry,* Winter, 361.
Gilligan, Carol. 1982. *In a different voice: Psychological theory and women's development.* Cambridge: Harvard University Press.
Mason, Mary Grimley, and Carol Hurd Green, eds. 1979. *Journeys: Autobiographical writings by women.* Boston: G. K. Hall.
Miyamoto Yuriko. 1980. Fujin to bungaku. In *Miyamoto Yuriko zenshu,* vol. 12. Tokyo: Shin Nihon Shuppansha.
———. 1962. *Miyamoto Yuriko shu.* Tokyo: Shinchosha.
Muramatsu Sadataka and Watanabe Sumiko, eds. 1990. *Gendai josei bungaku jiten.* Tokyo: Tokyodo Shuppan.
Showalter, Elaine. 1977. *A literature of their own: British women novelists from Brontë to Lessing.* Princeton, N.J.: Princeton University Press.
Tamura Toshiko. 1962. Miira no kuchibeni. In *Nihon bungaku zenshu.* Tokyo: Shinchosha.
———. 1987. *Tamura Toshiko sakuhinshu,* vol. 1. Tokyo: Tokyo Origin Center Shuppan.
Tanaka, Yukiko, ed. 1987. *To live and to write: Selections by Japanese women writers 1913–1938.* Seattle, Wash.: Seal Press.
Walker, Nancy A. 1990. *Feminist alternatives: Irony and fantasy in the contemporary novel by women.* Jackson and London: University Press of Mississippi.

FOUR

Transforming Business Data into Literature: Shimizu Ikkō's *The Artery Archipelago*

TAMAE PRINDLE

By and large, the major characters in and audience for the Japanese business novels (*keizai shōsetsu*) are men. Business novels, in this sense, are men's sagas or liturgies. Yet much of what transforms these business reports into literature is femininity. This essay examines how hard and dry information evolves into breast-heaving fiction in Shimizu Ikkō's *The Artery Archipelago* (*Dōmyaku rettō*).[1]

Part of the excitement generated by *The Artery Archipelago* results from its stylistic peculiarity as a cross between a business novel and a suspense novel. As a suspense novel, the archetypical "whodunit" plot structure ends halfway through, and the remainder takes the form of a "thriller."[2] That is, the protagonist's vulnerability pulverizes the reader's heart just as soon as the novelty of mystery solving wears off. But beyond the suspense and thriller, there is another literary agent, namely femininity, that facilitates our reading of the enormously dense and fascinating information about the Japanese Shinkansen, or "bullet train," system.

In this essay, Japanese names are given in the Japanese order, namely, the family name first.

[1] Shimizu Ikkō, *Dōmyaku rettō* (The artery archipelago) (Tokyo: Kadokawa Bunko, 1974). Numbers in parentheses are page numbers. All translations are mine.

[2] Todorov defines the "suspense novel" as a combination of a "whodunit" and "thriller" in that story number 2 (the story of the crime) takes central importance. For detail, see Tsvetan Todorov, *Introduction to Poetics* (Minneapolis: University of Minnesota Press, 1981), pp. 44–53.

Transforming Business Data into Literature 55

We may first note that *The Artery Archipelago*, like most business novels, offers encyclopedic information about technical matters. One passenger wagon, for example, weighs sixty tons. Since a train has sixteen wagons, its total weight reaches 960 tons. When this train hurtles along at 200 kilometers per hour, which is its average speed, its noise level rises to 150 phons. The resulting vibration loosens roof tiles and shakes houses built only a meter and a half from the track. Aggravating the situation, the trains pass Nagoya every five minutes.[3] Since the full capacity of the sixteen wagons is about fifteen hundred people and the Hikari (the name of one type of Shinkansen) is usually 70 percent full, approximately a thousand passengers would be killed in one accident if the train were overturned while cruising at its normal speed. The movement of each train is checked by the ATC (an automatic control device) as well as the CTC (the central control system). The former stops the train when a foreign object falls on the track; the latter evens out the spatial distribution of the trains.

Information extends to political matters also. The first Shinkansen service started in 1964, just before the Tokyo Olympics. The total length of tracks then was 515 kilometers. At the completion of the final plan, it will be about 7,000 kilometers, and the dense network of train tracks will spread throughout the Japanese archipelago as arteries do through the human body. Construction of the Shinkansen system is costly, but every added meter answers the prime minister's political desire to "reconstruct the Japanese archipelago" (58).[4] This type of information runs across the novel as the Shinkansen trains do across Japan. The Shinkansen pollution victims and the readers of the novel patiently watch them pass across their vision. Just as the technical information and the Shinkansen (the actual and the metaphorical) share the characteristic of dominance, so do the Shinkansen pollution victims and the

---

[3] Nagoya is southwest of Tokyo and between Kyoto/Osaka and Tokyo.

[4] *Nihon rettō kaizō* (Building a new Japan) was written by former Prime Minister Tanaka Kakuei, a strong supporter of the expansion of the Shinkansen network. Masamura states that this book was initially published as an expression of Tanaka's private opinion, but as soon as the Tanaka cabinet was formed, the book came to be read as the government's political goal. See Kimihiro Masamura, *Sengo Nihon shihonshugi-shi* (A history of postwar Japanese capitalism) (Tokyo: Nihon Hyōron-sha, 1983), p. 321. See also Kakuei Tanaka, *Building a New Japan: A Plan for Remodeling the Japanese Archipelago*, trans. Simul International (Tokyo: Simul Press, 1972). Although Tanaka's name is never revealed, educated readers can easily identify the prime minister in this novel to be Tanaka.

readers share the condition of passivity. And Akiyama Hiroshi, the protagonist, mediates between the two incompatible units. But as long as he defends the victims through "crimes," Akiyama becomes an accomplice of the pollution victims and the readers. This man does not obey the law of submission, however. Through rebellion, he awakens the public to the pollution victims' human rights and stimulates the readers' curiosity for more factual information. The more anxious the police become, the more meticulous their research becomes. The more meticulous is their research, the deeper involved we become in the technicality of the situation. Listen, for example, when the police and the railway staff discuss the first entry in Akiyama's list of demands:

> "How do you suppose he came up with the sixty phons for the noise level?"
> "Sixty?"
> "Yes, it's in the threatening letter."
> "As I recall, the suit by the group of plaintiffs from Nagoya was for below sixty-five phons."
> "So, this is five below it."
> "The national noise pollution law applies to over eighty phons. We can manage that easy enough, but below sixty-five is a tough proposition. The Shinkansen would have to run as slow as seventy kilometers per hour. At that rate, the Shinkansen won't be much faster than other trains. We'll be lucky if we can get three hundred fifty thousand passengers a day." (46–47)

The crime contextualizes the highly technical information.

In the sense that the Shinkansen system and its administrators work together, they constitute one part of a binominal equation; their victims are the other. The former group includes the staff of the railroad company, the police, a psychology professor who serves as a consultant for the railroad, and government ministers including the prime minister. *The Artery Archipelago* suggests that a monolithic power structure binds them together. Prime Minister Okeno controls, or at least intends to govern, his immediate as well as remote staff. Should anyone fail to obey his order, he screams vulgarities: *"Tsukamaero!"* (Go get the bastard!), *"Nanda to!"* (Bloody nuisance!), and *"Doitsu mo koitsu mo!"* (You good-for-nothing!) (207). He is "predatory" (*tsuyoki ni naru*) when it comes to the Shinkansen issue. It is not wide of the mark to say that the prime minister resembles the Shinkansen itself. He is generally impatient (*sekkachi*; 63, 107, 160, 203, 401) and is inclined toward spectacular display. A car is too slow for him. He is the major force behind the all-Japan Shinkansen network project: "What obstacles there may be, he would run through, by dint of his foolhardiness. To complete the rest of the all-Japan Shinkansen network was an important step toward Prime Minister Okeno's political goal, namely the reconstruction of Japan which will take as much as thirteen trillion yen" (58). The prime minister's single-track mind approximates the Shinkansen's linear motion and speed.

Other leading government officials also share the image of the Shinkansen. Their professional titles have affinity with the gloriously metallic rigidity of the Shinkansen. Kunimatsu Naoki is Director of the National Police Agency (Keishichō Chōkan). Akashi Yūsuke, who heads the investigation of the Shinkansen case, has the title Chief Clerk of the Special Investigation Committee No. 1 of the National Police Agency (Keishichō Sōsa Ikka Tokushu-han Sōsa Kachō). Culprit Akiyama's counterpart on the side of the political authorities, Takigawa Tamotsu, is Deputy Director of the Criminal Science Research Center of Police Science (Kagaku Keisatsu Kenkyū Hanzai Kagaku Kenkyūjo Fuku-Schochō). Far from mincing these harsh-sounding titles, the narrator underscores their importance by adding on lots of technical jargon written in Chinese ideograms, such as *seiji rinen tassei* (the materialization of the political ideology), *zenkoku Shinkansen-mō kōsō* (the nationwide Shinkansen network project), and *bakuhatsubutsu torishimari-hō ihan yōgi* (a suspected crime in light of the law concerning the administration of explosives) in explaining the activities and political goals of these government minions.

The characters' names also incorporate words like "upright," "maintenance," "guard," and "rock." Nagata's given name, especially, with *go* ("guard" or "protect") endorses its bearer's determination to complete the total Shinkansen network out of "national consciousness." These hard facts, names, titles, and phrases tightly structure the members of this community. This is the world of masculinity. In the words of Shima Yōko, a feminist who discusses women's problems from psychoanalytic standpoints, masculinity "privileges the analysis, classification, combination, and synthesis of pre-existing facts and finds value in the administration of principles which afford an objective recognition and conclusion."[5] In other words, the masculine world is an inflexible and principle-driven one, just like the Shinkansen itself.

---

[5] Shima Yōko, *Feminisuto saikorojō* (Feminist psychology) (Tokyo: Kakiuchi Shuppan, 1985), p. 74.

As might be expected, the female members of this community are castrated or, more in Hélène Cixous' line of thought, "decapitated."[6] They appear mentally or physically handicapped. Takigawa's wife, Michiko, is in the former category. Her puerility surfaces in her conversation with her husband on the Shinkansen Kodama. Following is her portion of the conversation:

"I wish I had bought tickets for reserved seats."
...
"...but the first wagon is the most dangerous."
...
"Are you sure it's safe? I mean even in the first wagon..."
...
"Does it mean it's absolutely safe?" (29–30)

True, the narrator interjects that Michiko spoke in the tone of trying to keep a conversation going rather than through true fear, but her husband doesn't miss the chance to put her down: "Women agonize over nothing" (29). It could well be that the problem stems from Takigawa's scorn for womankind altogether. Her name, Michiko, simply means "road," as if she were there to serve motorists and pedestrians. In counterpoint to the mentally handicapped Michiko, Nagata's wife is physically handicapped. Rheumatism confines her to her bed. These images of debilitated women are scattered throughout the novel like crumbled debris from a masculine typhoon. Somehow, this gender relationship reminds us of Freud's famous statement that libido belongs only to men.[7]

A woman simply caters to her spouse's needs. For convenience' sake, then, let us encapsulate all the qualities of the Shinkansen and its administrators in the term "masculine group." The Shinkansen, which resembles a phallus, symbolizes them all.

The other part of our binominal equation is Akiyama Hiroshi's circle, which we may call the "feminine group"; strictly speaking, Akiyama is more like a guest of honor in this group. This community is a breed apart from its hierarchically structured counterpart. Rather than subordinating or being subordinated by another, members of this community fend for themselves. Kimihara Tomoko has worked in the Nagoya Central Hospital with

---

[6] See Hélène Cixous, "Castration or Decapitation?" *Signs* 7, 1 (Autumn 1981): 41–55.

[7] For details, see *Sigmund Freud: The Complete Introductory Lectures on Psychoanalysis* (New York: W. W. Norton, 1966), p. 595.

Akiyama. Ochiai Fumiko is a college student majoring in economics and earns her living as a bar hostess at night. The third woman, Nogami Yasu, is Akiyama's seventy-four-year-old patient with heart trouble. She used to fend for herself by renting rooms in her house. The best explanation for these women's nonsubordination, perhaps, comes from feminist critic Luce Irigaray: "The issue is not one of elaborating a new theory of which woman would be the *subject* or the *object*, but of jamming the theoretical machinery itself, of suspending its pretension to the production of a truth and of a meaning that are excessively univocal."[8] The traditional gender-based classification of roles is not an issue to them.

The names of the three women suggest self-sustained equilibrium. Kimihara Tomoko means "noble-plateau knowledge." She is Akiyama's first aide and a "teller" who informs us about Akiyama and forecasts the consequence of his terrorism at the end of the novel. Fumiko, the name of the other woman, means "beautiful-lotus meeting." In Buddhist tradition, the lotus is associated with salvation. Fumiko's family name, Ochiai (which is rather common in Japan), is a play on the circumstance that Akiyama and Fumiko met (*ochiatta*) in a bar. Beginning with the 325-kilometer stretch between Tokyo and Nagoya, Fumiko drives Akiyama wherever he needs to go and puts him up in her apartment in Tokyo and in her friend's apartment in Nagoya. Akiyama's success depends very much on Tomoko's and Fumiko's help. Yasu means "peace" and Nogami means "above the plains." This elderly woman used to live "peacefully" by herself. These women do not live off men like parasites nor do they cater to any established political organization. In the sense that there is no monolithic power structure binding this group together, one might say that this is a naturalistic or philanthropic group.

The name of the "criminal" or "terrorist," Akiyama Hiroshi, means "broad autumn-mountain," meaning an uncontaminated Nature during the most sentimental season for the Japanese people. This naturalistic image is upheld at a metaphorical level by Tomoko's reference to the sleeping Akiyama as "a big log" and her reference to his "hairy chest," an animalistic image to a Japanese.

Voluntary trust and spontaneous affection, rather than political constraint, link the members together. Akiyama talks to Fumiko

---

[8] Luce Irigaray, *This Sex Which Is Not One*, trans. Catherine Porter with Carolyn Burke (Ithaca: Cornell University Press, 1985), p. 30.

at his first visit to her apartment:

> "Maybe you shouldn't have brought me here."
> "It's my pleasure to have you here."
> "But I am wanted by the police."
> "Oh?"
> ...
> "Can't you tell?"
> "Tell what?"
> "The T.V. program we watched at your bar."
> Tilting her head suspiciously, Fumiko looked Akiyama straight in the face. Perhaps grasping something, she hardened her expression slightly.
> "I don't mind leaving right now." Akiyama stood up.
> "Akiyama Hiroshi..., aren't you?"
> "Yes."
> "I couldn't tell."
> "I didn't mean to take you in with the name Minobe, but what else could I do in the bar?"
> "Your alias must come from Mino, your home country."
> "Something like that."
> "That's all right."
> "But this will put you in an awkward position."
> "I still don't mind. A friend of mine and I talked about you yesterday. We agreed that you are unquestionably impressive. It's exciting to meet you in person." (271–72).

It is Fumiko's decision to assist Akiyama.

Similar sympathy toward Yasu has triggered Akiyama's "terrorism." Tomoko's diary details his first encounter with the old woman, who was always frightened by something:

> First, Nogami Yasu complained of a kidney contraction and a heart disorder. She had an irregular pulse. The hospital's diagnosis was a hardening of the coronary arteries. The physician in charge gave her digitalis. But her tachycardia went from bad to worse. At a sign of fear, her pulse would increase to 170 or 180 per minute. Breathlessness and anxiety made a total captive of her.
> A direct current electric treatment was started at this point. (20–21)

Akiyama attributes Yasu's irregular pulse to the noise and vibration caused by the Shinkansen and makes up his mind to protest against the Shinkansen pollution. A man stands up to protect a woman, and other women volunteer to assist him. The members of this feminine group are bound by principles other than those of hierarchy and gender classification.

As the hidden architect of this egalitarian commune, Shimizu equips Tomoko with language that Lacan has reserved exclusively for men.[9] Tomoko's diary starts the novel and introduces Akiyama:

August 30, 00:00 o'clock
About half an hour ago, the eerie whistling of the shock waves caused by the Shinkansen to Tokyo passed through Nagoya City.
It got stuffier than expected tonight. I had only a glass of wine, but I feel drunk. This hypertension caused by intoxication keeps me awake. Because it is hot, also, I've been sitting in front of my desk ever since I got up to go to the bathroom. He is now sound asleep, looking like a big log that's been tossed on the ground. He is lying on my bedding in the four-and-a-half-tatami-mat room adjacent to this one.
It's been his habit since childhood to lie on his stomach. He says that he cannot sleep in any other way. But my bedding is only as wide as a Western single bed. (17)

This day's entry, ten pages long in the Japanese text, starts as a masculine text in the sense that it chronicles the date and time, but it soon waxes into a feminine one, not only because is it written by a woman and shows her helplessness, but also because it is written in a female language. It goes on to discuss a string of issues—Akiyama's bon-voyage party before supposedly leaving for Europe; a nurse's infatuation with Akiyama; Tomoko's own relationship with her former boyfriend and with Akiyama later on; her wonderment about Akiyama's sudden decision to take a trip to Europe; the latter's refusal to explain the decision; the case history of Yasu; Yasu's association of the Shinkansen's noise and vibration with her wartime fear of the American bomber, the B-29; the fact that 220 trips are made daily by the Shinkansen through Nagoya city between 6:25 A.M. and 11:36 P.M.; the pollution that makes it difficult to rent her apartment; the activities of the environmental protection group; her anxiety concerning a prospective marriage with Akiyama; her recollection of the time when he asked her to take out nitrogen; and finally a sense of relief felt at not having heard a report of an explosion. All these are written in a peculiar style where "the protagonist does not exist firmly at the center of the [text] like a Jamesonian center of consciousness, but instead, the story of herself becomes watered down by the stories

---

[9] See, for example, Cixous, "Castration or Decapitation?" pp. 45–46: "for Freud/Lacan, woman is said to be 'outside the Symbolic': outside the Symbolic, that is outside language."

of other characters."[10] This is what Cixous brands a "female text": "A female text starts on all sides at once.... What takes place is an endless circulation of desire from one body to another, above and across sexual differences, outside those relations of power and regeneration constituted by the family."[11] As the feminine group welcomes Akiyama into their unstructured community, so does Tomoko's text philanthropize and embrace everything indiscriminately. Giving women voices, voices that also keep track of masculine information but only in female terms, is Shimizu's way of dousing the hard-edged technical information.

The textual decentralization goes hand in hand with the women's political situation: no woman is a member of an environmental protection group. To underscore that the feminine group is a "peripheral" member of the political system at large, Shimizu pushes the habitat of the feminine group out of Tokyo to Nagoya. The headquarters of the masculine group is, needless to say, in Tokyo. This geographical layout stands as a metaphor of the Japanese gendered political power structure: men inhabit the "center" and women the "periphery." Women have never been a match for men.[12]

More metaphorically, Akiyama's social station is all but peripheral. Shimizu uses costume classification to illustrate this point. After dropping seven threatening letters into a mailbox at the central post office, Akiyama sees a group of young working girls in colorful uniforms. The narrator identifies him with these women who have no more importance than extras in a film or drama. Because his bright orange shirt matches theirs, the narrator

---

[10] Noriko Lippit, *Reality and Fiction in Modern Japanese Literature* (New York: M. E. Sharpe, 1980), pp. 192–93.

[11] Cixous, "Castration or Decapitation," p. 53.

[12] This dichotomy between cultural center and periphery has been discussed by Masao Yamaguchi, *Bunka to ryōgisei* (Culture and pluralism) (Tokyo: Iwanami Shoten, 1975), p. 106 et seq. Also see political scientist Susan Pharr's confirmation:

> The level of role strain experienced by political women in this study is vivid testimony to why so few women become politically active in Japan, despite the many changes that have occurred since women were granted full political rights after 1945. Except for the youngest activists, women in every age cohort from age eighteen to thirty-three confronted major constraints on their active political participation, and even the youngest activists were not altogether immune to role strain. (Susan J. Pharr, *Political Women in Japan: The Search for a Place in Political Life* [Berkeley: University of California Press, 1981], p. 168)

comments that "he did not look like an ordinary businessman no matter how one tried to justify him" (119). The shirt places Akiyama on the cultural "periphery." Another classification occurs with Akiyama's first letter to the prime minister. It is ranked "C" (the lowest priority); the prime minister does not even bother to look at the note his secretary has jotted down on it. Yet another indicator of periphery is the spot where Fumiko and Akiyama's former colleague fake Akiyama's suicide: in front of a monument commemorating Prince Omi no Okuni's death in exile.[13] The poem on the monument reads

> Clinging to this empty life,
> I hunt and eat the wild seaweed
> At the Irago Island,
> All drenched in the waves. (338–39)

The ancient prince had been deported by the government. Surrounded only by the ocean and wild seaweed, he was on the fringe between life and death. If this monument is not the landmark of the periphery, what else can be?

After proclaiming that the "center" is men's habitat and the "periphery," women's, Yamaguchi Masao instructs that the periphery is a region of multivalence:

> What's interesting is that our concepts find themselves in the center of our culture. The closer to the center, the more monolithic they are. On the other hand, because they are located outside our clear consciousness, the concepts about peripheral matters bear an ambiguity. Ambiguity means multivalence. To be ambivalent means that a word may superficially distinguish itself from another while maintaining a potential association with yet another word.[14]

Shima Yōko endorses Yamaguchi by replacing Yamaguchi's "multivalence" with a more psychoanalytic concept of "generosity":

> Female principle calls into question the male-principle-centered epistemology. It takes interest in the arena yet to be recognized as an objective truth and generously extends scientific curiosity to phenomena that have no clear-cut explanation.[15]

And Shimizu valorizes Yamaguchi's concept of multivalence in

---

[13] Prince Omi died in the eighth century. See *Man'yōshū*, vol. 1, poem 24, for the original.
[14] Yamaguchi, *Bunka to ryōgisei*, pp. 6–7.
[15] Shima, *Feminisuto saikorojō*, p. 74.

light of Shima's concept of generosity. Hence, the members of the feminine group cross over the traditional gender line to help each other.

So long as a political identity is neither a primary interest of the members of the feminine group nor instrumental to "terrorism," Akiyama tries to forsake it by fabricating a trip to Europe as well as a suicide. And the narrator assists Akiyama's effort to remain anonymous by calling him simply "a man" while he commits one of his crimes. The beginning of the eight-page episode reads as follows:

> A tall man with thick, black-framed glasses walks down the Shinjuku district office street from the direction of Shin-Ohkubo. Crossing over to the Isetan department store side of Yasukuni Street, where cars outnumber pedestrians, he heads toward the Sankō-chō intersection.
>
> He carries a small shoulder-bag in his hand.
>
> *Today may be another hot day,* he thinks to himself, looking up in the sky, where thin clouds floated, and pushing up with his index finger his slipping glasses. Thick, hairy arms protrude below his navy blue short-sleeve shirt. His pants and shoes are a matching color. The thin platinum necklace around his neck glimmers. (247–48)

The present-tense narrative places the "man" in a vacuum. Akiyama, a nameless substance, is scrutinized in terms of physical features and movements. Below the hot sun and thin clouds, he appears rootless and vulnerable.

To Shimizu, to be on the "periphery" means to suffer the consequence of the "center's" aggression. It is a vulnerable position. A telling scene in the first page of the novel backs up such a postulate:

> Under the intensity of the sun of late August—something to be called the last heat of the year—the scenery along the Tōkaido Shinkansen tracks expressed a lethargic, scorched fatigue; trees and grasses, and even hills and rivers, all gasped in suffocation. But the Shinkansen trains running about this time of the day, those numbered in the 400s, were not crowded, because they were extra runs; the cabin inspector moved about comfortably. (5)

The personified scenery is suffocating while the Shinkansen glides comfortably. This mapping symbolically exemplifies Yamaguchi's insight that "the closer to the center, the more monolithic [concepts] are." The farther removed one is from the center, the more vulnerable he or she is. This is why Yasu, the character probably farthest removed from the prime minister's political vision, is killed by the government's ad hoc Shinkansen policy. Tomoko's diary reports that

> in mid-June, after her return from the Central Hospital, as [Akiyama] had predicted, Nogami Yasu expired, attended by nothing but the constant noise and vibration that had kept whittling away her life for a long time and that had kept tormenting her. (24)

Yasu's fate is much the same as Prince Omi's.

It is obvious by now that the "crimes" that stimulate the reader psychologically are actually a challenge of femininity to masculinity. It takes the efforts of nonsubordination, self-sustained equilibrium, philanthropism, female language, periphery, vulnerability, and multivalence to break down the rigid masculine principles including the cut-and-dried technical information.

We witness in *The Artery Archipelago* how androgyny and multivalence fray the nerves of the inflexible masculine group:

> The police are capable of foreseeing, to a great extent, the gradual progress of the modes of crimes on the basis of past data. But they are unable to predict unprecedented and suddenly changing crimes. The latter are called metamorphic transformations. As an insect transforms from an egg, to a worm, to a cocoon, and then to an adult insect after repeated sheddings, the new forms have no resemblance to the previous ones. (103)

As "a woman can write her way out of the 'cramped confines of patriarchal space'" in a female text,[16] Akiyama's "crimes" can elude the police's predictions.

This shattering of the masculine principle by multivalence parallels the softening effect of the dry technical data. At the levels of both the plot structure and reader psychology, something like Richard Brown's "dialectical irony" or the "dialectical resolution of opposites" takes place, and "characteristically, A becomes B by avoiding B."[17] In opposing another, one becomes (like) one's opponent. Although the masculine and feminine groups fight against each other on the Shinkansen issue, each gradually imports the traits and syndromes of the other. The masculine group becomes increasingly conscious of and threatened by Akiyama. The feminine group's multivalence forces the police to aim their searchlight at "hidden unrequited victims" in symbolically peripheral regions. The symbolism is underscored when the

---

[16] Elaine Showalter, "Feminist Criticism," *Critical Inquiry*, Winter 1981, p. 201.

[17] Richard Brown, *A Poetic for Sociology: Toward a Logic of Discovery for the Human Sciences* (New York: Cambridge University Press, 1977), pp. 176, 177.

police begin to lurk in a tangerine orchard in the prefecture hitherto considered to be the pollution victims' habitat. As if to mix up the masculine and feminine indiscriminately, the police bring Tomoko to the orchard.

Akiyama, for his part, starts defending environmental concerns with the same doggedness that the president of the National Railroad, Nagata, has demonstrated: "He knew the difficulties involved in executing it under the police cordon, but the ecological problem was not to be solved unless he took the final step" (305). He pays a surprise visit to Nagata's house at night, scaring the railroad man like a child. And, lo, the "blood" starts "running" to Akiyama's side. Toward the end of the novel the terrorist steals a bloodmobile truck and drives it through the police-packed guard posts. It is as if the feminine group had responded to feminist Mary Daly's call to turn itself into a Be-ing, a verb, after so many years of hibernation as a nonbeing, a static noun.[18] The police fail to recognize the driver as Akiyama. They move to the side as if to turn themselves into a part of the scenery and let him pass. The figurative positions of the "center" and the "periphery" switch. Akiyama now takes the place of a Shinkansen, speeding through the gasping scenery. The criminal ceases to be a mere body but looms large as a thinking human being.

It is Tomoko who adjudicates the result of the power contest:

> "The bulldozer has fallen on the track as you have planned. This means that Prime Minister Okeno, who has sworn not to stop the Shinkansen service, has backed down along with the National Railroad. The Shinkansen service is stopped for the day. Mr. Akiyama, you did it. You stopped the Shinkansen on October first. You won." (439)

Tomoko is the only person in the novel who passes a clear judgment on Akiyama's effort. The author knows all too well that Akiyama's victory is an empty one: he concludes the novel with Akiyama's arrest, which follows Tomoko's declaration of his victory. A woman's verdict, of course, is an oxymoron by Lacanian definition. Even so, so long as the "periphery" or femininity is the torch-bearer of literary creativity, as Yamaguchi has pointed out, *it* must deliver the final verdict to make Shimizu's literary design work; men culturally constitute an established system, whereas

---

[18] Mary Daly, *Beyond God the Father: Toward a Philosophy of Women's Liberation* (Boston: Beacon Press, 1973), p. 34.

women "contrive, imagine, and create various dreams and deities."[19]

In summary, femininity in *The Artery Archipelago* operates at three levels: (1) to depict women as inhabitants of the socioeconomic "periphery," (2) to determine the style of Akiyama's "crimes," and (3) to stimulate reader psychology. The moment women step into the novel as fictional agents (as a diary writer, handicapped wife, Akiyama's aide, and so on), the discussion of technical information transcends facts and flies into the symbolic realm. And, of course, the symbolic realm is where "people transcend standardized regulations and definitions, and mobilize even their emotions to comprehend a hidden message"; it has the power to "directly link up a private microcosm and a conventionalized macrocosm."[20] We swallow femininity in our novel as a peptic that helps us digest the humanitarian implications of socioeconomic facts.

After turning the last page of the novel, we are left with a kind of euphoria at having learned something about the Shinkansen system and at having "produced" our own experience with the aid of the text. If Roland Barthes is right in saying that "the goal of literary work (of literature as work) is to make the reader no longer a consumer, but a producer of the text" and the Nobel laureate Ōe Kenzaburō in saying that it is the change in the psychological status of the characters that harnesses the activities of the readers' imagination at its full capacity,[21] we understand that *The Artery Archipelago* benefits from its articulation of femininity. The number of exchanges between the symbolic male and female approximates that between the text and the reader. One may conclude that Shimizu Ikkō has borrowed female identities to transform masculine business information into a piece of literature.

---

[19] Yamaguchi, *Bunka to ryōgisei*, pp. 127, 128ff.

[20] Ibid., p. 201.

[21] Roland Barthes, *S/Z*, trans. Richard Miller (New York: Hill and Wang, 1974), p. 4. Ōe Kenzaburō, *Shōsetsu no hōhō* (Method of novels) (Tokyo: Iwanami Shoten, 1978), p. 81.

FIVE

The Identity in the Carpet

CRIS REYNS

> It was something, I guessed, in the primal plan; something like a complex figure in a persian carpet. He highly approved of this image when I used it, and he used another himself. "It's the very string," he said, "that my pearls are strung on!"
>
> Henry James, *The Figure in the Carpet*

In 1988, John Whittier Treat, a specialist in atomic bomb literature, wrote, "A recent poll of leading Japanese intellectuals revealed *Black Rain* as the majority choice for the most significant book in Japan since 1945" (1988, 199). Ibuse Masuji's *Black Rain*[1] is still a "best seller" in the 1990s, both in Japan and in the United States, even though it is a difficult book to read. It is difficult first because it deals with a horrible suffering of human beings, implying if not guilt, at least a feeling of either heavy responsibility or unbearable fatality. But *BR* is also difficult because its literary form is complex. So why does the ordinary Japanese still read it? There seem to be two main reasons, which correspond to two different groups of readers: For critics of the media, it is a matter of content, that is to say, the description of ordinary Japanese life after the explosion of the bomb; for academics, it is the extraordinary richness of the literary forms. It is this plurality of readings that interests me and that I attempt to explain in this essay.

Every reader who approaches the book, whether in Japan or in the United States, knows that it is a book about the atomic bombing of Hiroshima. Because no one particular form seemed satisfactory to represent that devastating event, Ibuse used the old forms in a different way. It is not an exaggeration to say that Ibuse took

---

[1] Hereafter referred to as *BR*. All quotations from John Bester translation. All names are cited in the Western order. Emphasis is mine except where otherwise noted.

most of them and put them together brilliantly. The result of this literary collage is puzzling, and we can say that *BR* goes beyond the representation traditional in A-bomb literature; it is also a questioning of the traditional form, a way to contest the traditional representations of any similar event, or even more generally of the "real."

Many have written on the Hiroshima-Nagasaki bombings, but often in quite traditional forms (Yoko Ota, Tamiki Hara, John Hersey, etc.). For Ibuse, the idea of writing about Hiroshima was not new either; he had already published a short story on the subject, "The Crazy Iris," in 1951. It took him twelve more years to write *BR*, by far his longest and most ambitious narrative. Ibuse said that he came back to that subject as a reaction against the numbing folklorization of the horror through rallies, TV documentaries, and the like. One of his characters in *BR* says, "Everybody's forgotten! Forgotten the hellfires we went through that day—forgotten them and everything else, with their damned anti-bomb rallies. It makes me sick, all the prancing and shouting they do about it" (29–30). This exasperation was shared by many, including non-Japanese such as Marguerite Duras (1960, 11), who said in the synopsis of *Hiroshima mon amour*, "One of the major aims of the movie is to put an end to the description of horror by horror, because this has been done by Japanese themselves, and instead to make this horror rise from its own ashes."[2]

The problem of memorializing victims' sufferings has become an ongoing contemporary challenge, intellectually and ethically, in many parts of the world (the most obvious being the Nazi Holocaust, but we know there are many others). For most critics, *BR* is a Japanese or world "memorializing" narrative. In *A Critical Study of the Literary Style of Ibuse Masuji*, Anthony Liman gives an interesting explanation of the Japanese "Shintoist" attitude toward the memory of the dead: "For the age-old Japanese attitude toward the souls of the dead never stresses merciful forgetfulness, but on the contrary, clear remembrance. The memory must be carried on, be it ever so painful for the survivors" (457–58).

Speaking about the victims of the atomic bombing, many critics fall into the trap of essentialism, reinforcing the Japanese feeling of uniqueness. As for any human suffering, the question is neither

---

[2] My translation of "Et c'est là un des desseins majeurs du film, en finir avec la description de l'horreur par l'horreur, car cela a étèt fait par les Japonais eux-mêmes, mais faire renaître cette horreur de ces cendres."

Are we able to reproduce the essence of the Japanese suffering? nor Are we morally allowed to do it?³ but rather *How* can we represent such an event? This "how" implies not only a technical, here literary, challenge, but also a political and ideological problem.

In contrast to his colleague Ōe Kenzaburō, Ibuse is famous for his noncommitment in life and his noncommitted literature. But we know that politics affects everyone, even those who don't care about politics. Therefore my concern here is with the possible takeover of this "neutral" *BR* by nostalgic ideologies. I think that the context for Ibuse's narrative, which is the Japanese conscious or unconscious use of the idea and feeling of victimization, reinforces the interpretation of Japan's uniqueness and maintains therefore an ideology of isolation.

But what in the text would allow this interpretation of uniqueness? First, Ibuse presents the bomb as a natural disaster: "At Furue there was a great flash and boom. Black smoke rose up over the city of Hiroshima *like a volcanic eruption*" (17). Comparisons like this are numerous in the book, reinforcing the "naturalness" of the title *Black Rain*. Ibuse also believes that nothing can be done to change history. Consequently a certain fatalism hovers over the story. As he says in *Waves*, quoting Du Fu, "Nations fall, but rivers and mountains remain." Hence Ibuse describes his characters as paying extreme attention to the details of everyday life, just as he as a writer does to the textual details.

Paradoxically, Ibuse, the advocate of the ordinary Japanese life, was, like modern Japan itself, very influenced by other countries.[4] I will not insist here on the biographical proofs, such as that he studied French literature in the 1920s in Tokyo, already a very internationalized city. Ibuse could not but have been aware of the many international, then dominantly Western, literary ideas.

---

[3] Although Theodor Adorno recanted ten years later (see "Perennial suffering has as much right to expression as a tortured man has to scream; hence it may have been wrong to say that after Auschwitz you could no longer write poems" [1994, 362]), he first said in 1957 that to write poetry after Auschwitz is barbaric (1967, 34).

[4] The paradox is between an obvious intellectual way of writing (the working with or on the forms) and the content, which tends to be interpreted as nonintellectual, if not anti-intellectual. For more about this anti-intellectual perspective, see Treat's *Writing Ground Zero*, 261–77. Although Ibuse never said anything explicitly about himself as an intellectual, he would probably define himself more as a humble artisan (see his anti-elite statements, quoted in Liman 1992, 466).

Although he kept his distance toward any literary and political movements, it can be shown that he was influenced by the craze for Tolstoy at the beginning of the century, the proletarian pro-Marxist literature of the 1920s, the French existentialist literature of the 1940s, the French *nouveau roman* of the 1950s, and the American documentary novel of the 1960s. Hence it can be said that he knew about their nonlinear or antilinear narratives, as well as their eschatological or antiteleological histories.

This is obvious in the text itself. Ibuse's narrative is a complex weaving of this international intertextuality with Japanese traditions. BR weaves different genres, different types of discourse, and different voices (such as the more Western omniscient voice; see Fowler 1988 and Fujii 1993) with the diary, a more Japanese genre (see Miner 1969; and the journals of Shigematsu, Shigeko, Yasuko, Dr. Iwatake, and others). But it also interbraids pieces of Japanese mythological stories (see the myth of Tanabata [233]), references to popular tales (see the stories of Momotaro [44] and Pinocchio [233]), and wild tales and rumors with references to high culture such as to Lady Murasaki, and in a more Western documentary style, references to menus, personal messages, legal notices, and so forth.

The first result of this weaving of literary genres is to contest naive literary realism. Ibuse, with a cruel humor of his own, suggests what would be the only "real" news item of the documentary: "'Awful! I caught it, all right.' He turned around to show me. The skin of his back had come clean away from his shoulders and was hanging limply, like a piece of wet newspaper" (79).[5]

Moreover, these woven voices are rarely given in one block, but more often in pieces, distributed in regular intervals, in a way that if we consider each discourse as a thread, the metaphor of the tapestry or the carpet appears clearly. When I say "clearly," I do not refer to a realistic representation.[6] In fact, in a very interesting reversal, it is as if Ibuse presented the back of the tapestry to his readers and hid the front, with the clear image.[7]

---

[5] This allusion to the newspaper could be read also as a parody of newspaper "realism" itself.

[6] Interestingly enough, although Ibuse is also a painter, there is no reference to images in this text, except once (but it is cruelly ironic; BR, 89).

[7] Hence my title. See also the contrast between Ibuse's "unfinishedness" and Shigematsu's obsession of "copying cleanly" (*seisho suru;* Treat 1988, 211) and exhaustively.

In effect readers see the seams, the knots of the text. The ordinary reader sees the "back yard" of everyday Japanese life. Academics see the process of researching but also the work in process itself, the spinning of the yarns from the basic material, such as superstitions, rumors, and the personal diaries throughout the literary work. Ibuse presents his readers an unfinished work and a story with no ending (we do not know about Yasuko's health at the end).

The first advantage of this alternation among the voices is the relativization of all of them, including to some extent the omniscient narrator's voice and Shigematsu's obsession with exhaustiveness.

The second advantage of this technique is to break the monotony. Each part could by itself become monotonous: the monotony of horror with its accumulation of descriptions of horror that would be eventually numbing, but also the monotony of the everyday life in the country, and even the monotony of the weakly plotted double narrative of Yasuko (her arranged marriage and her health).

The third advantage is that it allows Ibuse to contrast these discourses to amplify their effects: to contrast the abstract deadly bomb with the concrete country life; to contrast the city with the country; to contrast the two recent pasts (the military one [1930–45] and the days of the A-bomb), with the "olden days" (premilitary even pre-Meiji), and also with the two presents (Shigematsu's present [1950s] and the present of writing-reading [1960s]). The suture points between the pieces of the Japanese "quilt" are sometimes smoothed through techniques such as a key word or key theme like the pool of water connecting chapters five and six (84–86). But most of the time the seams are readily apparent, creating a break that strikes some as a "defect," creating the feeling of an "unfinished work."

After all this, it is difficult to call BR a clean, clear, traditional novel, what some critics, after Michael Bakhtin, would call a monological text, that is to say, a text with one dominant ideological voice. On the contrary, the interbraided text shows Ibuse's clear opposition to any official version of History or Truth, including the Japanese state ideology, both the prewar imperialist one and the postwar industrialist one:[8] "If only we'd been born in a country, not a damn-fool state," says one of the characters (162).

---

[8] See his his satire of the army and even of the emperor in BR (11, 45).

This interweaving makes *BR* a good example of what postmodern critics see as positive because it is antimetanarrative, hence antitotalitarian. Bakhtin was one of the first literary critics to develop this theory. In many ways Ibuse's narrative could be defined as Bakhtinian: it is indeed parodic, popular, carnivalesque, and polyphonic.[9] This polyphony is created and creates the feeling of "unfinishedness" described above, which Bakhtin dialectically relates to modern society: "[this novel] best of all reflects the tendencies of a new world still in the making, the novel is a genre in the making" (1990, 11).[10]

However, my interpretation differs. To make clear my explanation, I am going to distinguish two concepts that are usually presented as synonymous by Bakhtin and his critics. Although I agree that *BR* is polyphonic, that is to say, "a [diversity] of independent and unmerged voices and consciousness, a genuine polyphony of fully valid voices," I do not agree that it is dialogic, that is to say, open. I see this polyphony in *BR* reduced to a monological discourse, which is the nostalgia for an ideal Japanese small community or village, such as Awane-Kamo, where Ibuse was born, and Kobatake, where Ibuse's protagonists live after the explosion of the bomb.

This reduction to a monological discourse can be best seen in the pervading metaphors of natural space. By insisting on spatial metaphors, Ibuse shows one more time that he repudiates not only the linear story, but linear history as well. In *BR*, history is not like the Western, Christian, Hegelian line (and even less like the Marxist progressive line), wherein human beings are agents weaving their story. It is more a natural history, wherein people are passive, accepting the natural laws and the hierarchical rules, also believed to be natural. So in some way it is possible to read this philosophy as a typical Japanese way of seeing history.[11] If *BR* does not present a negation of temporal development, its temporal development is subsumed within the natural space.[12]

---

[9] For Bakhtin, the carnivalesque is not a question of (un)happy events, but a way to see life, including death, such as in the *danses macabres*. In *BR*, beyond death, Ibuse affirms life as the supreme value. The carnivalesque does not reject any human or living act such as farting, defecating, or the like. For example, see in *BR* the description of "dirty" themes: sex (211), underwear (147), feces (99, 159, 173), etc.

[10] See Bakhtin: "The sole genre that continues to develop and has no canon of its own and parodies other genres, and has this ability to criticize itself" (1990, 3–11).

[11] There are very few articles in English on that subject. See Wilson 1980.

[12] Ibuse had already experimented with this technique of subsuming the tem-

These metaphors pervade the texture of *BR*, and here I shall briefly analyze four networks: weaving, fishing, writing, and relating.

Because Japan is an island country with very little agricultural land, fishing is a basic activity. For centuries, and until very recently, fish was, with rice, one of the main foods:

> At supper time the previous day, Yasuko had said to him sympathetically, "Going to inspect the ponds is a kind of act of homage for you, isn't it Uncle? I don't expect it's such fun as it looks to the outsider." But she was wrong: it was a pleasure that no outsider could possibly know, a pleasure comparable to that of fishing. (26)

After this passage the fishing leitmotiv appears regularly, often in counterpoint with the description of death and horror from the bomb. But what I want to highlight here is first the association of the fishing net with another net that is described in terms that make it essential:

> Taking some bricks from where the wall had collapsed, I loaded them on the *mosquito net* and a parasol to sink them. The net was a valuable piece of property that could be traded *for 50 go of rice*, and I weighted it. (86)

Second, note that the recurrent image of the fishing net takes the pattern of a grid. The same obsessive image of the grid recurs in various ways with the theme of textiles,[13] first through the theme of the clothes like the ones sent in anticipation of a disaster:

> [A]nd [we] went home to get our belongings ready for sending to the country. List: Aunt Shigeko's summer and winter formal kimonos. (16–17)

The textile motif also shows how essential textiles are to protect people, even a victim of the bomb, as in the case of Shigematsu's neighbor:

> His face was ashen but unscathed. I assumed he had been caught in a fire and got his back burned by flames, but I was wrong. Early that morning, he had gone to call on an acquaintance who lived somewhere within sight of the keep of Hiroshima Castle, and had been taking off his polo shirt before going inside.... He had

---

poral within the spatial several times, especially in his short story "The River" (Treat 1988, 61–73; and Liman 1992, 205–31; see also Liman's interesting mythopoetical analysis of time-space images in *BR*, [1990, 490 passim]).

[13] Although weaker, the English word "net" in the sense of "text, texture, fabric, and social fabric" does exist also in Japanese; see *hensho suru*.

been hurrying, he told me, and was soaked in sweat. But just as he got the shirt over his head there was a terrifying roar and flash. His head and face were muffled in the shirt. (79)

Because of where the three protagonists go, the motif then takes on a special dimension. We remember that Shigematsu after some wanderings in the devastated city meets his wife and then his niece. They want to go home but their house is burning. Then, strangely, Shigematsu decides to cross the city to go with them to his factory, the Japan Textile Company (95). In itself this trip across the city could be interpreted as a narrative necessity: some people, sane and educated, had to cross the "hell" (160) to be able to retell "objectively" what and how it was. But Ibuse could have sent his characters somewhere else—for example, to a cannery—or given the factory another name. Moreover, Ibuse has the boss of the factory send Shigematsu through that hell again to the other side of the city to get coal so that the factory can go on producing clothes.[14]

These textual facts are reinforced by the historical context of the production and reception of the book in the 1960s. It is not necessary to explain how essential the textile tradition was in Japan.[15] To show how this tradition was still important as a leitmotiv in Japanese literature in the 1960s, it is sufficient to refer to *Kyoto*, the "novel" that Kawabata published in 1962, in which he shows the decline of the traditional textile workshops.[16]

The third net appears in the importance placed on the material of Japanese traditional writing: *washi* (Japanese paper), calligraphy, Chinese ink and brush. Each of these tools can be seen as one more sign of the "grid" that almost any Japanese reader would recognize. First, the *washi* shows clearly the traces of the rods on what is called "laid paper" in English, and therefore the reader can see the grid pattern in the paper itself. Second, contrary to the Western tradition, the writing is usually vertical and right to left, although it could also be horizontal, left to right. These two ways of writing and reading create a mental image of the grid.[17] In the same way, the insistence on using Chinese

---

[14] Ironically, the army refuses to give permission for the coal that would be used to produce those clothes made for the army.

[15] Reischauer (1964) confirmed this interpretation, giving it a broader, more directly and explicitly political context (1964).

[16] I base my interpretation of that novel upon Etiemble 1980.

[17] For the Western reader, the parallel with theories about spatial reading superimposing upon linear reading, from structuralism through deconstruction, is a way

(black) ink on white paper, if put in parallel with the black rain of the title, could be interpreted as a way to insist on that grid pattern through the kanji "rain":[18] "I suddenly remembered a shower of black rain... and the rain from then had fallen in streaks the thickness of a *fountain pen*" (34). If I add to this the fundamental kanjis related to the meaning "field," the kanjis of the rice paddies, present in the name of the village (Kobatake) where the protagonists live, all present everywhere and in so many names in Japanese, we see that this pattern is almost obsessive.

All these textual nets reinforce the image of the grid pattern as a way for Ibuse (mainly unconsciously) to reaffirm the supremacy of the eternally good village, the social fabric in an eternal nature, over a conception that would favor historical transformations. If Ibuse does not share the official conception of hierarchy in Japanese society, he shares with many Japanese[19] the nostalgic idea of a community-village that never existed in this idealized "natural" harmony.

It is not necessary to insist too much on the fourth grid pattern, the image of the social fabric. Anthropologists have shown extensively how Japanese traditions, customs, and rituals wove a complex and rich network. Ibuse describes how the bomb ripped this social fabric and shows how essential it is to patiently mend it. Ibuse himself contributes to this reweaving by textually interconnecting the four networks. For example, writing is connected to the social through Ibuse's insistence in *BR* on the importance of the mail in Japanese society:

---

to understand this idea. Ibuse could have known about these theories since Japan was closely following the "Western modes" (see Ishida 1989). Numerous French writers used that grid as a voluntary constraint on their writing as early as the 1960s; see Motte 1984.

[18] "In the West the movement of rain is mainly seen as vertical but the heavy rain in Japanese can be 'legs'—*ama-ashi*—and a rain can be a 'rising rain'—*yuudachi*" (Liman 1992, 496–97). This connection between the fountain pen and the black rain also implies that the countries from which these two "bad" Western products come are themselves "bad," "decadent" countries—see Pat Dowell, "*Black Rain:* Hollywood Goes Japan Bashing," *Cineaste* 17, 3 (1990): 8–10—reinforced by the fact that after page 44, the pen will be explicitly despised as a Western artifact. Shigeko insists on using Chinese ink because it lasts longer (40–43). Ironically, in Japanese, the pen is called *man'en hitsu*—that is, "ten-thousand-year brush"!

[19] And non-Japanese; see Anderson 1983, and see also the notion of community from Plato to Kant to Heidegger. For a more literary point of view, see Bhabha 1990; and for French cases, among many, see a writer such as J. Giono under Vichy France.

"According to mother, letters first started coming to the villages in the sixth year of Meiji," said Shigeko. "They were sent care of somebody in Kukuyama or Okayama, then they were given to somebody to bring from there." (42)

The old man had still been working as a mail carrier for Kobatake post office in those days. Every day for more than twenty years, come rain, come shine, he had gone to and fro with the mail on his back between the Kobatake and Takafuta post office. The minister of communications had even given him an award for his services. (74-75)

Writing is subtly connected to fishing in this quotation:

It's nothing to do with theories. From a literary point of view, the way I describe things is the crudest kind of realism. By the way, have these [carp] been kept in clean water long enough to get rid of the muddy taste? (60)[20]

Finally, all of these nets are related to the main leitmotiv, the bomb: the bomb is related to fishing (the mushroom cloud of the bomb is compared to a jellyfish [34]); second, the bomb is related to clothing (the atomic cloud has a "texture" [53]); third, the bomb is related to social fabric (crowds are compared to "swirls, whirls, tidal waves" [57]); and fourth, the bomb is related to writing (which is supposed to be the only remedy against the effects of the bomb itself).

Hence I conclude that even though the polyphonic dimension in BR is the result of numerous influences—Japanese, Western, traditional, modern, popular, and "pure literature"—and several competing discourses, without any will to obtain a political synthesis, nevertheless it is eventually reduced to a monologic subtext: the communitarian ideology.

To support this interpretation I quote from David Pollack's *Reading against Culture*, speaking about Ōe Kenzaburō, who is Ibuse's contemporary:

The problem remains, we realize, that history cannot simply be rewritten "as one wishes it to be." Having accepted this rationale for arbitrary closure, Oe abandons his archaeological methodology, sealing off its problematically ambiguous multiple possibilities. Unable to reduce competing realities to the truly aleatory, however, *The Silent Cry* finally takes refuge in notions of blood roots

---

[20] The change of theme in the conversation is strikingly sudden and could suggest a parallel between theory and mud, between cleaned fish and the "crudest kind of realism."

springing from the soil, the unique discourse of race, and a mythology of communal mediation of conflict. Although he seems to be speaking against such essentializations of culture, Oe seems trapped by the sorts of essentialist reactions to the problems of modernity which have become the subject of recent Western criticism. Far from any "postmodern" resolution of the boundaries constituting the problem, this criticism observes instead a stubborn tendency in Japanese thought, postwar as well as prewar, to reject the very idea of "modernity" itself as something originating in (and plaguing) the West and therefore essentially alien. (208–9)

My interpretation of *BR* as monological is even reinforced by the absence of certain themes or characters. Although Ibuse gave voice to the poor Japanese in some of his stories—that is, the voices of the nonordinary, middle-class, male Japanese—the voices of the independent woman, Eta, Ainu, and more obviously of the Foreigner are textually absent.[21] My point is that by getting rid of the Foreign, the Other in *BR*, Ibuse reinforces the feeling of "one (is)land / one nation / one religious feeling / one language." This creates an ambiguous feeling of uniqueness, in this case a uniqueness in victimization.[22] It gives the impression that for Japanese, the Other is almost more dangerous than the bomb.

An oft-noted tendency in Japanese history is to borrow foreign products (material or cultural) and adapt them to native "philosophies."[23] In *BR*, as we have seen, Ibuse borrowed many foreign literary and ideological components, but he integrated them into a Japanese philosophy in which time is natural and cyclical more than historical and progressive and in which it is subsumed by space. I gave several examples to indicate that the village was a

---

[21] Strangely enough, protagonists in *BR* do not use insults, concrete names, or personalized appellations for the American enemies. It looks like self-censorship to me (for racist insults in American war novels, see Johnson 1991). The American seen as an Enemy is here an abstract threat on the order of those in Poe's fantastic tales (I am thinking of "The Red Death," for example). In fact, foreigners are almost completely absent in those three hundred pages (in the six days of the diaries and in the five or six years of the story), although we know that many foreigners lived in Hiroshima, especially Westerners, Catholics, and Protestants, but also Koreans and other minorities.

[22] This feeling is comparable to the one stated by certain Jewish critics about the Holocaust, prolonging the "chosen people" ideology. It forgets that millions of homosexuals, Gypsies, Slavic people, and others were also killed because they were not "pure, normal, decent" Aryans.

[23] I intentionally use the plural, since in spite of the official version, there are various ideologies in Japan (Shintoism, Buddhisms, Confucianisms, Socialism, Liberalism, etc.).

kind of space that was nostalgically re-created for the ideal community of "pure ordinary Japanese."[24] Inasmuch as this village-community can easily be interpreted as a metaphor for the whole of Japan,[25] it is not an exaggeration to fear that this image implies a national(istic) feeling, helped by a strong old-new extratextual *nashonarizumu*.[26] That is why I have insisted so much on these spatial metaphors. My purpose is not to refute the view of the many critics who commented upon a neutral, nostalgic "beautiful Japan and Ibuse,"[27] but to unveil what could be interpreted as a compromising ideology—one with which ordinary Japanese readers identify and "scientific" academics refuse to deal.[28]

I would like to conclude with a more positive interpretation. First, if Ibuse's BR is not dialogic, it is clearly polyphonic, displaying an extraordinary textual richness.[29] Second, BR is protected against any possible easy takeover by conservative or reactionary movements by the fact that what is affirmed here is not state nationalism, but, let us call it, "country nationalism."[30] Third, the tone has nothing to do with a strong or simplistic glorification, but is closer to a modern Japanese "pastoral" of a peaceful nation.[31]

---

[24] For a historical explanation of the importance of the village in Japanese mentalities, see Fukutake 1982. Many Japanologists speak about "village vs. city" as a main theme in Japanese literature. Ibuse's three main critics (Kimball, Treat, Liman) extensively pursue this line of criticism about Ibuse's works.

[25] Hiroshima could also be interpreted as a metaphor for Japan as the big island (Hiro-shima) "bullied" (50) by the bomb/Foreigner. See the "sinking Japan" in the translators' introduction to "The Isle-on-the-Billows" (113); see also Napier 1994.

[26] *Nashonarizumu* is the Japanese version of nationalism; see Reischauer, 91–92.

[27] See (in Pollack 1992, 4) Kawabata's Nobel Prize speech "Japan the Beautiful and Me" (trans. E. G. Seidensticker) and how it was used by the National Japanese Railway Company.

[28] For this move from a prescriptive critique to an "objective" critique refusing to deal with ethical and political problems, see Siebers 1988.

[29] This international intertextuality makes the narration more difficult to identify with the nation, even if the nation, as in the Japanese case, is stereotypically presented inside (see *Nihonjinron*) and outside ("Japan, Inc.") as monolithic and monologic (one emperor, one [is]land, one language, one people).

[30] The word "country" refers here as much to village as to *kuni*, but it could also be called "community-nationalism"; see Treat 1995, 275 .

[31] "For the most part pastoral tends to be an idealization of shepherd life, and, by so being, creates an image of a peaceful and uncorrupted existence.... Though pastoral may die in one form it is likely to be reincarnated, and the traditional primitivist themes reanimated. To support this, one may cite the novels of Jean Giono" (Cuddon 1991). See, for example, Vergil's pastoral, *Georgics*, but also his epic, *Aeneid*, reinterpreted by Herman Broch in a political context (see "La Fiction et Auschwitz, H. Broch et M. Blanchot," *L'esprit créateur* 24, 3 (1984): 57–67).

Finally, I would like to insist that in many literary fictions, as opposed to clearly ideological essays for example,[32] it is difficult to discern the degree of openness because it depends so much on the readers' historical context, knowledge, and, eventually, will. So whether or not Ibuse's book will eventually be interpreted as a nostalgic, conservative narrative is difficult to say.[33] Therefore, let us interpret Ibuse's nostalgia as a nostalgia for another kind of reading, similar to the one Peter Brooks finds in Walter Benjamin's "Storyteller" essay: "What Benjamin would wish to restore, or to create, is perhaps most of all a certain attitude of reading that would more closely resemble listening, that would elicit the suspension of meditation rather than the suspense of consumption."[34]

References

Adorno, Theodor W. 1967. *Prisms*. Trans. S. Weber. London: Spearman.

———. 1994. *Negative dialectics*. Trans. E. B. Ashton. New York: Continuum.

Anderson, Benedict. 1983. *Imagined communities*. New York: Verso.

Bakhtin, Michael M. 1990. *The dialogic imagination*. Trans. Caryl Emerson. Austin: University of Texas Press.

---

[32] I am thinking of the *Nihonjinron* or the essays of the Kyoto school in the 1930s, or even of the second Eto Jun (see Ishida 1989).

[33] Because of this polyphonization, *BR* could be called a postmodern text. But this contradiction between a dialogic form and a monologic content proves that critics (such as L. Hutcheon) who present postmodern writing as always deconstructing metanarrative are much too optimistic. A precise historical recontextualization is necessary. The changes in Shohei Imamura's filmic interpretation of Ibuse's *BR* are a good proof of that necessity. Made in 1988 in the middle of the internationalization obsession and fashion (*kokusaiteki na*), this more international medium presents a less obvious nationalistic village voice. To give only one example, Yasuko is not any more only a passive object in the *o-miai* process; she has become a more Westernized subject, choosing her lover herself.

[34] Brooks 1994, 87 (although my final proposal is not without a paradox: asking the reader to have an active reading of this story and at the same time to accept the passive reading of History in *BR*).

Bhabha, Homi K. 1990. *Nation and narration.* New York: Routledge.
Brooks, Peter. 1994. *Psychoanalysis and storytelling.* Cambridge: Blackwell.
Cuddon, J. A. 1991. *A dictionary of literary terms.* Oxford: Blackwell.
Duras, Marguerite. 1960. *Hiroshima mon amour.* Paris: Gallimard.
Etiemble, René. 1980. *Comment lire un roman japonais.* Paris: EIBEL.
Fowler, Edward. 1988. *The rhetoric of confession.* Berkeley: University of California Press.
Fujii, James A. 1993. *Complicit fiction.* Berkeley: University of California Press.
Fukutake, Tadashi. 1982. *The Japanese social structure.* Trans. R. P. Dore. Tokyo: University of Tokyo Press.
Ibuse, Masuji. 1969. *Black rain.* Trans. J. Bester. Tokyo: Kodansha International.
———. 1985. "The crazy iris." In *Fire from the ashes.* Trans. A. Liman, ed. Ōe Kenzaburō. Tokyo: Readers International.
———. 1987. *Waves.* Trans. D. Aylward. Tokyo: Kodansha International.
Ishida Hidetaka. 1989. "Situation du langage dans la critique littéraire au Japon." In *Littérature japonaise contemporaine,* ed. P. DeVos, 151–66. Bruxelles: Labor.
James, Henry. 1970. "The image in the carpet." In *Stories of writers and artists,* ed. F. O. Mathiessen. New York: New Directions.
Johnson, Sheila K. 1991. *The Japanese through American eyes.* Stanford, Calif.: Stanford University Press.
Liman, Anthony V. 1992. *A critical study of the literary style of Ibuse Masuji.* Lewiston: Mellen.
Miner, Earl. 1969. *Japanese poetic diaries.* Berkeley: University of California Press.
Motte, Warren. 1984. "Georges Perec on the grid." *French Review* 57, 6: 820–32.
Napier, Susan J. 1994. "Panic sites: The Japanese imagination of disaster from Godzilla to Akira." *Journal of Japanese Studies* 19, 2: 327–51.
Pollack, David. 1992. *Reading against culture.* Ithaca, N.Y.: Cornell University Press.
Reischauer, Edwin O. 1964. *Japan, the story of a nation.* New York: Knopf.

Siebers, Tobin. 1988. *The ethics of reading.* Ithaca, N.Y.: Cornell University Press.
Treat, John W. 1988. *Pools of water, pillars of fire.* Seattle: University of Washington Press.
———. 1995. *Writing ground zero.* Chicago: University of Chicago Press.
Wilson, Macklin G. 1980. "Time and history in Japan." *American Historical Review* 85, 3: 557–71.

SIX

Discernment or Volition: Linguistic Politeness Strategy in Japanese

SHOJI AZUMA

Our speech behavior is constrained by variables such as situation, hearer, and topic, which both individually and in combination formulate how we compose various types of utterances in differing degrees of politeness. For example, a simple request to someone to sit down can be framed in differing levels of politeness. Some of the variants in English are given in (1).

(1) a. Sit down.
b. Will you sit down?
c. Won't you sit down?
d. Could you sit down?
e. You'd be more comfortable sitting down.

Sentence structure—imperative, interrogative, declarative—as well as modal verbs and tense can convey different degrees of politeness to a hearer. A competent native speaker can associate a certain linguistic form with a linguistic need arising in interpersonal relations between a speaker and a hearer. The issue of linguistic politeness has become the focus of research in sociolinguistics and allied fields beyond the level of table manners and etiquette.

Brown and Levinson (1978, 1987) have proposed one of the most influential theories of linguistic politeness as a cross-linguistically universal theory (see also Lakoff 1975, Leech 1983). Brown and Levinson (1987:56) "identify strategic message construction as the key locus of the interface of language and society" and argue that speakers employ various politeness strategies to save "face" in conducting a face-threatening act (FTA). According

---

I would like to thank Peter Nosco for comments and Junko Kawashima for assistance in data collection. Needless to say, all shortcomings are mine.

to them, "face" is the desire of every competent adult that his or her actions be unimpeded by others or that his or her wants be desirable to at least some others. The FTA intrinsically threatens face. It includes requests, orders, suggestions, warnings, offers, promises, compliments, criticism, and disagreement, among others. For example, a request threatens the hearer's desire to be unimpeded by the speaker, and thus a rational speaker will employ a particular politeness strategy to mitigate the threat. Observe the following example:

>   (2) I know you can't bear parties, but this one will really be good—do come!
> (Brown and Levinson 1987:125)

According to Brown and Levinson (1987), one politeness strategy is to assert or presuppose the speaker's knowledge of and concern for the hearer's inclination. In (2), by saying that the speaker knows the hearer does not like parties, the speaker asserts knowledge of the hearer's inclination and exhibits willingness to fit his or her own wish with that of the hearer's.

Ide (1989) argues that the theoretical framework of Brown and Levinson (1978, 1987) is inappropriate when languages with honorifics—like Japanese—are examined. According to Ide, in addition to the intentional politeness strategies such as that in (2), which were the main focus of Brown and Levinson (1978, 1987), linguistic politeness can be accomplished by simply obeying society's prescribed norms as in the case of honorifics in Japanese. Observe the following examples:[1]

>   (3) *Sensei-wa   kore-o   yonda.
>   professor-TOP   this-ACC   read
>
>   (4) Sensei-wa   kore-o   o-yomi-ni-natta.
>   REF. HONO. PAST
> (Ide 1989:227)

The sentence in (4) has a referent honorific *o ninat*, which is used in referring to the action of a professor, who is of high status in Japanese society. According to Ide (1989), the sentence in (4) is appropriate but the sentence in (3), which does not have a referent

---

[1] * indicates that the sentence is ungrammatical. In glossing the Japanese examples, the following abbreviations are used: ACC=accusative; REF HONO=referent honorific; TOP=topic.

honorific, is inappropriate in Japanese society, suggesting that the honorific verb form is sociopragmatically obligatory. The speaker cannot actively choose a linguistic form as an intentional strategy, but simply has to choose the socially prescribed form. Ide (1989) argues that the Japanese practice of polite behavior according to social conventions, which she calls *wakimae* or "discernment," is the neglected aspect in Brown and Levinson's framework, which mostly deals with the "volitional" aspect (which allows the speaker a considerable active choice among available linguistic codes in polite behavior).

As a proof of how prevalent this discernment aspect of polite behavior is, Ide and her colleagues (Hill et al. 1986) conducted a comparative study in which Japanese and American subjects were asked to choose from a list of expressions, which differed in their degree of politeness, those that they would use to request a pen from various categories of people (e.g., professor, department store clerk, co-worker, close friend). The results were striking: there was a clear correlation between the expressions and people categories for Japanese subjects, but not for American subjects. For example, Japanese chose polite forms like *Kasite itadake masen ka?* (May I borrow a pen?) as an appropriate form to people of power or people socially distant from the subject (e.g., a professor), but not to people of less power or people socially close to the subject (e.g., a co-worker). Less polite expressions like *Kasite* (Lend me) were chosen as an appropriate form for people of less power or people socially close to the subject (e.g., a co-worker), but not for people of power or people socially distant from the subject. This pattern was uniformly observed. For American subjects, the distribution of responses was very broad, and there was no compartmentalization. For example, expressions such as "Can I use...?" were used for almost all the categories. It appears, then, that there is no socially prescribed absolute form to be used exclusively for specific groups of people in English, while in Japanese there are such socially prescribed forms.

Given the results of the study, we can say that the discernment aspect of politeness seems to prevail far more in Japanese than in English. An interesting question then is, What is the magnitude of the discernment aspect in the Japanese context? Is it powerful enough to override the volitional aspect of polite behavior? To be more specific, when faced with a serious FTA (i.e., high degree of imposition), does a Japanese speaker still comply with the socially prescribed polite forms or does he or she make an active choice?

A particularly interesting question in such a scenario concerns linguistic behavior toward people who are socially powerless or distant from the speaker. Does he or she still use less polite forms even when the degree of imposition is very high?

Method

The present study used questionnaires. Forty-three Japanese university students in Japan were told to assume that they were student teachers in a secondary school and that they were about to ask two kinds of addressee, a teacher (person of power and socially distant to subjects) and a student (person of less power and socially close to subjects), to open the window for them. All of the subjects were enrolled in a teacher-training program at the university and were to face the situation as part of their graduation requirement sooner or later. It was thought that giving them a relevant situation to respond to would elicit responses close to their actual speech behavior.

There were two parts in the questionnaire: one situation in which the addressee was not engaged in any activity (part 1), another in which the addressee was busy engaging in some activity (part 2). In both situations, subjects were asked what they would say depending on the addressee: teacher or student. Part 1 (low imposition) was expected to elicit the most unmarked response from subjects and was also considered to be a replicate of Hill et al. (1987). Part 2 (high imposition) was considered as the marked situation in which the risk of imposition by the request was very high because the addressee was preoccupied with some other activity. The FTA of the request in part 2 was considerably more imposing than that of part 1. To minimize unnecessary linguistic variations, all subjects were asked to start their utterance with *mado-o akete* 'open window' and to end with their choice of appropriate forms differing in the degree of politeness.

In part 1, we would expect to observe compartmentalization—polite forms to a teacher and less polite forms to a student, resulting in the replication of Hill et al. (1987)—if discernment is the prevailing concept among Japanese as was claimed in Ide (1989). In part 2, we would continue to observe the same compartmentalization if discernment overrides volition. The use of the same polite forms to both a teacher and a student—a result of the mitigation of the highly imposing FTA—would suggest that discernment does not override volition.

Results and Discussion

Tables 1–4 (pp. 92–93) show the results of the study. There are several interesting findings in part 1. First, all utterances are compartmentalized; no single utterance is chosen for both addressees. For example, the utterance *mado o akete kureru* was chosen as an utterance to be used only to a student, never to a teacher. Similarly, the utterance *mado o akete itadake masu ka* was chosen as an utterance to be used only to a teacher, never to a student. No single utterance was used in both situations. Second, all of the polite utterances chosen were used to a teacher, not to a student, and all of the less polite forms were used to a student, never to a teacher. Utterances in table 1 (to a teacher) all have the *masu* morpheme, which is a polite form in Japanese. Furthermore, honorific humble morphemes such as *kudasai-* and *itadake-* are also included. On the other hand, the utterances in table 2 (to a student) have neither *masu* nor honorific humble morphemes, and the utterances are characterized as less polite or plain forms. Some of the subjects (N=5) chose the bare gerundive form *akete*, which is considered the least polite form. The overall pattern of the responses in part 1 shows linguistic compartmentalization, resulting in the replication of Hill at al. (1987). The results in part 1 show that *wakimae* 'discernment' is indeed persistent among native speakers of Japanese as Ide (1989) argues.

The situation in part 2 is one of high imposition, because the addressee is engaging in some activity when the request to open a window is made. Tables 3 and 4 show the utterances chosen in part 2. The major finding of part 2 is that the linguistic compartmentalization in part 1 also shows up in subjects' responses even under the highly imposing situation. The utterances to a teacher (table 3) are all polite forms characterized by the polite *mas-* morpheme suffixed to *akete*, while the utterances to a student (table 4) do not have the polite *mas-* morpheme; instead, the plain morpheme of *kure* 'give me' is suffixed. The imposing nature and seriousness of the FTA, however, triggered subjects to choose more polite forms than the forms in part 1 for both the teacher and the student addressee. For example, some of the subjects added phrases of apology such as *sumimasen ga* 'I'm sorry but' or *yorosikere ba* 'if you don't mind' to their utterances to a teacher (N=11).

Only a few (N=2) added phrases of apology such as *chyotto* 'a little' or *gomen* 'excuse me' to their utterances when speaking to a student. Thus, the seriousness of an FTA indeed influences a subject's utterances.

It is important to note, however, that even in a serious FTA the subjects chose less polite forms for students than for teachers. For example, the polite form of *mado o akete kudasai masen ka* was used only in to-a-teacher situations, never in to-a-student situations. The plain form of *mado o akete kurenai* was used only in to-a-student situations, never in to-a-teacher situations. We see, then, the same kind of clear compartmentalization in part 2 as we saw in part 1. Even the imposing nature of the FTA did not influence subjects' discernment: subjects did not choose the polite forms in table 3 when speaking to a student.

To summarize, the questionnaire study revealed that the discernment aspect of politeness is indeed persistent among Japanese native speakers (part 1) and that this discernment is not canceled by the seriousness of an FTA (part 2). Subjects did not maximize the volitional aspect or intentional aspect of politeness by choosing some of the polite forms in a to-a-student situation to mitigate the imposition of the FTA. What subjects did was to conform to socially prescribed forms, thus maintaining *wakimae* even in a serious FTA. The interesting finding is this persistent nature of discernment among Japanese speakers.

One aspect of discernment is to use polite forms to those who have more power or are socially distant. An apparent shortfall to this discernment, from the Western egalitarian viewpoint, is the poor treatment of those who have less power or are socially close. An interesting question is whether the seriousness of an FTA would elevate the degree of politeness equally to both those who are powerful or distant and those who are powerless or close. The results in part 2 suggest that the seriousness of an FTA maximally benefits those who are powerful or distant (e.g., a teacher) and minimally those who are powerless or close (e.g., a student). For example, comparing the results in part 1 and part 2, we notice several changes in part 2:

1. The number of polite utterance forms for to-a-teacher situation increases from 5 different utterances to 9, but there is no significant increase in the to-a-student situation (from 5 utterances to 6).
2. Polite forms of apology are added to utterances in to-a-teacher

situations (N=11), but only plain forms of apology are added in to-a-student situations, and then only by a few (N=2).

Most subjects make their utterances more polite in the to-a-teacher situation in part 2 than in part 1, but they are not that enthusiastic in doing so in the to-a-student situation. In fact, several subjects asked the investigator if they were obliged to change their utterances in the to-a-student situation in part 2; they did not find any necessity to change their utterances in the to-a-student situation from part 1 to part 2, as they had in the to-a-teacher situation. Thus, the seriousness of an FTA does not equally increase the level of politeness across the two addressee situations. Only the teacher as addressee benefits from the seriousness of an FTA. In other words, mitigation to the FTA is appropriate to an addressee who has more power or is distant from a speaker, but not as necessary to an addressee who has less power or is close to the speaker.

This finding offers an interesting implication to the universal theory of linguistic politeness of Brown and Levinson (1989). According to them, an FTA can be done baldly without redress (i.e., no mitigation) in circumstances where (a) face demands can be suspended in the interest of urgency or efficiency, (b) the FTA is in the hearer's interest, and (c) the speaker is "vastly" superior in power to the hearer. The relevant circumstance here is the last one. The question is, What kind and magnitude of power relation between speaker and hearer can cancel the mitigation requirement for an FTA? In the Japanese context the power relation is static rather than dynamic, in the sense that such a power difference is socially prescribed and not obtained through dynamic interpersonal negotiations of right and obligation occurring between speaker and hearer in discourse. Members of Japanese society are constantly making a decision about the power difference between an addressee and themselves in their speech. The difference could be large (e.g., doctor and patient) or small (e.g., neighborhood store clerk and customer); the important point is that the magnitude of the difference is irrelevant as long as the difference exists. Thus, in the Japanese context, the power difference does not have to be "vast" for doing an FTA baldly without redress. If so, the characterization of "vast" power difference implied as universal in Brown and Levinson (1987) must be adjusted to accommodate the Japanese situation.

Implication

The present study confirmed the hypothesis that *wakimae* (i.e., complying with social conventions) is the important aspect of politeness in the Japanese context (Hill et al. 1987, Ide 1989). Furthermore, it was shown that in a serious FTA, discernment is intact while volition is kept minimal and does not override discernment. The study further suggests that in an FTA, linguistic mitigation or redress is more likely to be done toward those who are powerful or distant than to those who are powerless or close. If we use cultural anthropology's concepts of *uchi* 'in-group member' and *soto* 'out-group member' and associate those who are powerless or close to a speaker with *uchi* and those who are powerful or distant from a speaker with *soto*, then Japanese speech behavior of politeness might be summarized as "maximize your redress to *soto* members and minimize your redress to *uchi* members."

Let's consider the results of this study in the light of cross-cultural communication between English and Japanese. The finding that in the Japanese context the discernment aspect is far more important than the volitional aspect even in a serious FTA offers an important cultural insight for English native speakers when they communicate with Japanese verbally or nonverbally. For example, how is an English native speaker treated by Japanese in the Japanese context? If the Japanese views the English native speaker as powerful or distant from the speaker (i.e., a *soto* member), the Japanese would treat him or her with very polite linguistic behavior, often too polite from the English native speaker's view. On the other hand, if the Japanese views the English native speaker as powerless or close to the speaker (i.e., an *uchi* member), the Japanese would likely treat the English native speaker with plain or bald linguistic behavior, often rude from the English native speaker's viewpoint. Such behavior could puzzle the English native speaker: Japanese are extremely polite, but sometimes they are extremely rude. The answer to this paradox is simple: Japanese are neither extremely polite nor extremely rude; they are simply manifesting their way of being polite according to their own system of politeness. Thus, English native speakers should not be upset or puzzled when they see a Japanese being very "polite" in one instance and very "rude" in another. It is not, in fact, considered rude to speak to one's *uchi* member in plain or bald forms in an FTA. Quite the contrary: speaking plainly or baldly without redress to one's *uchi* member is a socially acceptable, even a "nice" or "friendly" speech style. Conducting an FTA baldly without redress is a symbol of solidarity with one's *uchi* member. In English, however, it is not considered "nice" or "friendly" to conduct an FTA baldly without redress, even to an *uchi* member. If the Japanese pattern is carried over when a native Japanese speaks English, a native English speaker would probably consider the speech to an *uchi* member as rude and the speech to a *soto* member as excessively polite or formal (Azuma 1994). Thus, for native Japanese speakers, it is important to know that in the English context, redress to an FTA is necessary to one's *uchi* member as well as one's *soto* member.

If such customs are not borne in mind on both sides of the language divide, communication is hampered even if the language is understood.

References

Azuma, S. 1994. *Teinei na eigo shitsurei na eigo*. Tokyo: Kenkyushu.

Brown, P., and S. Levinson. 1978. Universals in language usage: Politeness phenomena. In *Questions and politeness*, ed. E. N. Goody, 56–289. Cambridge: Cambridge University Press.

———. 1987. *Politeness: Some universals in language use*. Cambridge: Cambridge University Press.

Hill, B.; S. Ide; S. Ikuta; A. Kawasaki; and T. Ogino. 1986. Universals of linguistic politeness: Quantitative evidence from Japanese and American English. *Journal of Pragmatics* 10:347–71.

Ide, S. 1989. Formal forms and discernment: Two neglected aspects of universals in linguistic politeness. *Multilingua* 8, 2/3: 223–48.

Lakoff, R. 1975. *Language and women's place*. New York: Harper and Row.

Leech, G. 1983. *Principles of pragmatics*. London: Longman.

Table 1
Subjects' utterances to a teacher
and their frequency in part 1

Utterance	Frequency (N)
mado o akete itadake masu ka	18
mado o akete itadake masen ka	11
mado o akete kudasai masen ka	7
mado o akete morae masu ka	4
mado o akete kure masen ka	3

Table 2
Subjects' utterances to a student
and their frequency in part 1

Utterance	Frequency (N)
mado o akete kureru	16
mado o akete kureru ka na	11
mado o akete kure nai	9
mado o akete	5
mado o akete yo	2

Glosses for the Japanese utterances in tables 1 and 2:
mado	'window'
o	accusative
akete	gerundive form of 'open'
itadake	honorific humble form of *morae* 'I humbly receive'
masu	formal auxiliary
-ka	question morpheme
masen	*mas-*=formal auxiliary, *-en*=negative
kudasai-	honorific humble form of *kureru* 'give me'
morae-	'receive'
kure-	'give me'
-na	tag
-yo	tag

Table 3
Subjects' utterances to a teacher and their frequency in part 2

Utterance	Frequency (N)
mado o akete itadake masen ka	11
mado o akete itadake masu ka	10
sumimasen ga mado o akete itadake masen ka	8
mado o akete itadake nai deshyō ka	5
mado o akete kudasai masen ka	4
yoroshikere ba mado o akete itadake masen ka	1
mado o akete morae masu ka	1
mado o akete itadaki tai no desu ga	1

Table 4
Subjects' utterances to a student and their frequency in part 2

Utterance	Frequency (N)
mado o akete kureru	15
mado o akete kureru ka na	14
mado o akete kure nai	9
mado o akete kure nai ka na	3
mado o akete kure nai	1
chyotto mado o akete kureru	1

Glosses for the Japanese utterances in tables 3 and 4:

sumimasen-ga	'excuse me, but'
deshyō	'will'
yorosikere-ba	'if you don't mind'
-tai-	'want'
-nodesu	'as you know'
-ga	'but'
gomen	'I'm sorry'
chyotto	'a little'

SEVEN

The Interface of Two Cultural Constructs: *Kotodama* and *Fūdo*

ANN WEHMEYER

The Japanese language has been viewed as being infused with *kotodama* 'word spirit' since antiquity; the earliest use of the term itself is found in the three instances of its mention in the songs of the *Man'yōshū* (ca. 759).[1] Scholars have delineated three major stages in the evolution or permutation of what was understood to be the nature of *kotodama* over time, from the *kotodama* faith (*kotodama shinkō*) or the animistic belief of the archaic period in the power of the spoken word to effect reality, to the view in the Heian and Kamakura periods of *kotodama* as the power of beautiful words to enable communication between men and gods via poetry, and finally to the *kotodama* ideology (*kotodama shisō*) of the Edo period, when the vitality of *kotodama* had perhaps died out as a working belief or aesthetic, and scholars turned to rediscovering what was meant by the reference to Japan as "a land blessed by the spirit of words" in the *Man'yōshū*.[2]

I gratefully acknowledge the research support of the Japan Foundation for work on this project.

[1] Songs 5:894, 11:2506, 13:3254.

[2] The phrase occurs in a *chōka* by Yamanoue Okura (?660–?733), song 5:894, dated 733, first portion only given here (Takagi Ichinosuke, Gomi Tomohide, and Ōno Susumu, eds., *Man'yōshū*, 2:102–103; translation from Ian Hideo Levy, *The Ten Thousand Leaves*, 390):

Kamiyo yori	It has been recounted
iFitute keraku	down through time
sora mitu	since the age of the gods:
Yamato no kuni Fa	that this land of Yamato
sume kami no	is a land of imperial deities'
itukusiki kuni	stern majesty,
kototama no	a land blessed by the spirit of words.
sakiFaFu kuni to	Every man of the present
kataritugi	sees it before his eyes

The Interface of Two Cultural Constructs 95

The conceptualization of *kotodama* as the "divine structure" of the Japanese language by early nativist scholars such as Keichū (1640–1701), Kamo no Mabuchi (1697–1769), and Motoori Norinaga (1730–1801) provided a strong impetus for investigation of the grammar and sounds of the Japanese language. In their philological study of Japan's earliest texts and their ancillary analyses of the grammar and sound structure of Japanese, we find the beginning of linguistic science in Japan. We can in fact find in the writing of Edo- and Meiji-period nativist scholars approaches to the analysis of language that have much in common with both ancient and modern approaches to the analysis of language in the West.[3] It is in the last major "school" of the nativist movement, that of *kotodama* studies (*kotodama-gaku*), that we find theories about the origin of human language. The *kotodama* studies school was formed by a peripheral group of religious scholars who regarded themselves as heirs to the methodology of the theory of the sound-meaning school (*ongi-setsu*). It is in their work that we find an interface with what I will argue is a salient feature of Japanese cultural identity, that of *fūdo*, or the association of person and being with place.

---

iFitugaFikeri   and knows it to be true.
ima no yo no
Fito mo kotogoto
me no maFe ni
mitari siritari

[3] A representative sample of areas investigated, authors, and their respective works is listed here:
  a. grammar (morphology)
    i. verbal conjugation: Kamo no Mabuchi (*Go-i*, 1769)
    ii. *kakari musubi* (agreement between emphatic particles and verbs): Motoori Norinaga (*Teniwoha himo kagami*, 1771; *Kotoba no tama no wo*, 1785)
  b. phonology
    i. distinctive sounds: Keichū (*Wajishōranshō*, 1695)
    ii. sound-meaning theory (*ongi-setsu*): Takahashi Zanmu (*Kotodama no yado*, 1841); Suzuki Shigetani (*Kotoba no chikamichi*, 1845); Togashi Hirokage (*Kotodama yūgenron*, 1868); Hori Hidenari (*Ongi zensho*, 1913)
  c. "God-Age script": Hirata Atsutane (*Kanna hifumi den*, 1819)
  d. philology/hermeneutics: Motoori Norinaga (*Kojiki-den*, bk. 1, 1790)
  e. cognitive linguistics: naming, Fujitani Nariakira (*Ayuishō*, 1773)
  f. literary interpretation: Fujitani Mitsue (*Kojiki tomoshibi*, 1808; *Makoto-ben*, 1804–1808)
  g. origin of human language: *Kotodama-gaku* school: Nakamura Takamichi (*Kotodama wakumon*, 1834); Ōishigori Masumi (*Dai Nihon kotodama-gaku*, 1903)

This essay has a twofold purpose. The first is to suggest that the work of Watsuji Tetsurō (1889–1960) on the role of climate in shaping the formation of culture, which looms as a landmark of twentieth-century thought, may be placed on a continuum with the development of the concept of *fūdo*, a term ostensibly borrowed from the Chinese, within Japanese culture. The second purpose of the essay is to provide a case in point that complements the work of Watsuji, that of the interface of the two concepts of *kotodama* and *fūdo*, in the work of those in the school of *kotodama* studies.

A logical starting point for discussion of the term *fūdo* is the five regional gazettes extant among those commissioned by Empress Genmei in 713, which only came to be known by their present-day titles of *fudoki* some two centuries later.[4] Although these texts are presumed to have been modeled on some form of regional Chinese gazette, there are only a few Chineses texts given the title of *fengtu ji* (J. *fudoki*) in the Chinese historical records.[5] The reports commissioned by the Empress Genmei were originally titled *ge*, a term indicating a report submitted by a subordinate to a superior. Akimoto notes that in Kamakura period commentaries, these reports are given the descriptive title of "*fudoki* texts" (*fudoki no bun/fumi*) and suggests that the term represented a spontaneous coinage based on everyday terminology rather than an official title.[6] It therefore appears that what was borrowed from the Chinese was merely a technical term referring to "weather and soil conditions," which was subsequently expanded in the context of Japan to refer not only to geographical features and local production, but also to regional customs and regional lore.

The work of Watsuji and of his contemporaries Nishida Kitarō (1870–1945) and Miki Kiyoshi (1897–1945) is often discussed in juxtaposition with Western thought—in particular, in the context of their work as endeavors to fill in the "gaps" they perceived in Heidegger's thought. Watsuji's own account of his realization of

---

[4] Aoki Michiko Yamaguchi, trans., *Izumo fudoki*, 25; Akimoto Kichirō, "Kaisetsu," 7.

[5] A reference to one is found in the *Jin shu* (Aoki, *Izumo fudoki*, 25n5). The biography of Zhou Chu states that he wrote a *fengtu ji* (*Jin shu*, 5:58.1569–1574, Zhonghua shuju edition, 10 vols. [Beijing, 1974], 1571). Zhou Chu hailed from Wu, but served in military office in Luoyang, capital of Western Jin. There is also a text containing the term *fengtu ji* in the *Shuo fu* collectanea: a Yuan dynasty account of a foreign country titled *Zhenla fengtu ji* (4: 2623–2650).

[6] Akimoto, "Kaisetsu," 8.

the importance of *fūdo* for the analysis of human character and behavior is given precisely in this context.[7] Recent work of Dale, however, has brought to our attention the fact that the "climatic" approach to the analysis of culture did not commence with Watsuji. Dale points to Shiga Shigetaka's (1863–1927) *Fūkeiron* (1894) as the first work in this vein in Japan.[8] The work of the religious scholar Usami Keidō (b. 1895) also antedates Watsuji's *Fūdo* by several years and argues that *kikō-fūdo* 'climate and natural features' are key factors in the origin and development of language.

In the work of Usami, *kotodama* represents the "spirit of words" in the sense that sound, and words composed of sounds, are a distillation of an emotional or mental state.[9] The key to interpretation of meaning, therefore, is to identify the particular mental state or emotion expressed by an individual sound. He uses the following reasoning to explain his premise: the word *koe* 'voice' is a contraction of the phrase *kokoro no e* 'the essence of the heart';

---

[7] Watsuji's inspiration was Heidegger's *Zein und Seit* (1927), which he read in Berlin in 1927:

> I found myself intrigued by the attempt to treat the structure of man's existence in terms of time but I found it hard to see why, when time had thus been made to play a part in the structure of human existence, at the same juncture space also was not postulated as part of the basic structure of existence.... I perceived that herein lay the limitations of Heidegger's work, for time not linked with space is not time in the true sense and Heidegger stopped short at this point because his *Dasein* was the *Dasein* of the individual only. (in Watsuji Tetsurō, "Preface," v)

[8] Peter N. Dale, *The Myth of Japanese Uniqueness*, 41. Minami Hiroshi identifies Shiga's *Fūkeiron* as the first work linking geographical and climatic features to the formation of the character of the Japanese people as a nation (*Nihonjinron no keifu*, 46–47). He notes that it was published in the year of the outbreak of the Sino-Japanese War and suggests that Shiga's remarks that the Japanese landscape was blessed with a beauty of which it could boast to the world and that the tastes and culture of the Japanese people living within this natural environment were highly refined were of great interest to the people of Japan at the time, given the heightened national consciousness. In his consideration, however, of the history of the tradition within Japan of linking cultural characteristics to geographical factors, he points to an earlier work, *Jinkokuki*, published in 1701 and compiled by Seki Motohira (dates unknown), as the first work in this vein (40). The work surveyed the regional history, culture, and practices characteristic of the people in thirty-five provinces and suggested that the character of a people, like that of plants, is determined by the watering of the soil. Minami does not, however, trace the genre back to the *fudoki*, as I am suggesting here.

[9] Usami Keidō, *Nihon kotodama-gaku gairon*, 4ff. Originally appeared in *Nihon oyobi Nihonjin*, January 1932.

accordingly, some mental function always underlies vocalization via *kotodama*.

Usami suggested that the origin of human language lay in vocalizations that were expressions of instinct, such as *sakebigoe* 'exclamation' (literally, "exclaiming voice"), *nakigoe* 'crying', and *waraigoe* 'laughing', and that these spontaneous vocalizations later became codified into words and parts of speech. Such spontaneous vocalizations were determined by what he called *kikō-fūdo* 'climate and natural features'. This is the point at which cultural particularism appears. Although the phenomenon of *kotodama* itself is universal, Usami argued that it was harnessed in its purest form in Japan because of the particular natural environment of Japan, which allowed for the creation of sounds in their "pure" form (*seion*). Japan, being neither a torrid nor a tropical zone, does not have the diphthongs or "assimiliated" sounds characteristic of, for example, polar regions.[10]

Usami eschewed the methodology of comparative linguistics, which sought to establish genetic relationships among languages based on sound-correspondence and to account for sound change over time by, among other things, dispersement of population over distant geographical areas. Rather, he argued, languages share what appear to be similar words or cognates as a result of their spontaneous origin conditioned by climate and natural features. One example of such apparent cognates he discusses is the word for "fire" in various languages, such as *fire* in English, *pyr* in Greek, *ho* and *hi* in Japanese, and *fuo* in Chinese. These words, he claims, are all based on sounds from the "ha-line" of the syllabary, or various fricative consonants, because the sounds represent the feeling of warmth generated from putting the palm of the hand in front of the mouth and blowing on it.[11]

The major focus of the school of *kotodama* studies lay in the elucidation of the meaning of individual sounds and in this respect did not differ from the goal of the investigation of sound and determination of sound-meaning taken by the school of sound-meaning (*ongi-setsu*) in the late Edo and Meiji periods. Although proponents of the school of sound-meaning also attributed the meaning of sound to a divinely bestowed *kotodama*, the methodology was not so different from that adopted in the comparative method, namely, the identification of sound and meaning

---

[10] Ibid., 5, 19.
[11] Ibid., 13–14.

similarity to delineate the roots or morphemic building blocks of language. The methodology adopted by the school of *kotodama* studies, on the other hand, represented an a priori assumption of seventy-five mental or emotional states, corresponding to the "seventy-five letters of the syllabary,"[12] and consisted of construction of etymologies by collecting and comparing words that seemed to be expressive of such mental states. The two approaches may be compared by examining the attempts of both schools to clarify the inherent meaning of the sound /o/.

The school of *kotodama* studies believes that the sound /o/ indicates "spirit" (*seishin*) and that the words in which it appears indicate various permutations of "spirit" derived through what they call the "conjugations" added to the sound /o/, as in the data below:[13]

osoreru	'to fear'	(the spirit leaves the body and gravitates to another)
odoroku	'to be surprised'	(the spirit thunders; *otodoru* 'to thunder')
obiyakasu	'to frighten'	(the spirit chills and shortens)
obieru	'to be afraid'	(the spirit shrinks and feels nightmarish)
osou	'to attack'	
odokeru	'to joke'	(the spirit is induced to lack control for a period of time)
okoru	'to anger'	(the spirit contracts and is not easily undone)

The theory of sound-meaning approach, by contrast, and as exemplified in an exhaustive treatise by Hori Hidenari (1819–1899), the *Ongi zensho* (1913), categorized each sound according to what were considered its "five functions," or broad semantic classifications. The classifications seem to represent groupings based on similarities of meaning that have no relation to any pre-set notions of what sort of meaning could be codified

---

[12] The term "seventy-five letters of the syllabary" is taken from the esoteric arrangement of the sounds of the Japanese syllabary, including the voiced and /p/ versions, found in the chart called *masumi no kagami*, discovered in Kyoto by Nakamura Takamichi. The chart, and a discussion of its interpretation, may be found in the Kaisetsu-hen (27) companion volume to Ōishigori Masumi, *Ōishigori Masumi zenshū*. Discussion of this aspect of the school of *kotodama* studies appears in the latter part of this essay.

[13] Usami, *Nihon kotodama-gaku gairon*, 20–21.

by sound. The sound /o/ in its "five functions" (broad semantic classifications) is analyzed as follows. In some instances, comparison is made with words containing the vowel /a/, which seem to represent an antonym:[14]

1. 'to go down, settle down'
   oriru 'to go down'   vs.   agaru 'to go up'
   oku 'to place'   agu 'to raise'
   oto 'younger brother'   ani 'older brother'
   otoru 'to be inferior'
   otiru 'to fall'
   oyogu 'to swim' (implies "sink")
   oboru 'to be drowned'

2. 'to get narrow'
   oku 'interior'   vs.   aku 'to open'
   oi 'aged'
   osoru 'to fear'
   odaFi 'to be relaxed and calm'
       subset: 'a dark phenomenon'
   oboro 'hazy, clouded'
   oroka 'stupid'; 'trifling'

3. 'heavy things'
   omoi 'heavy'
   osu 'to push'

4. 'to sprout down' (?; no examples)

5. 'arising'
   okoru 'to anger'
   oFu 'to bear'
   okoru 'to arise'
   oFo 'big'
   oFo 'numerous'

At this point it is useful to compare the interpretation given to the characterization of Japan in the *Man'yōshū* as "a land blessed by the spirit of words" in each of the two schools. In the school of *kotodama* studies, interpretation is grounded in the belief that "climate and natural features" determine sound, and thereby the origin of language. In this view, Japan is a land blessed by the spirit of words precisely because its natural topography allows for the generation of sound in its purest form. Countries not so blessed

---

[14] Hori Hidenari, *Ongi zensho*, 1:54ff.

could not harness *kotodama* so transparently. Usami also maintains that the sounds of the Japanese language have undergone fewer changes over time than other languages. He argues, therefore, that the true meaning encoded by sound in the indigenous vocabulary of Japanese may be applied to foreign languages as well to elucidate the inherent meaning of words in those languages.[15]

The school of sound-meaning, on the other hand, in defining the meaning of "a land blessed by the spirit of words," focuses on the definition of "spirit of words" (*kotodama*) and states that *koto* refers to the *gen* 'word' of *gengo* 'language' and thus indicates "the words of people" (*hito no kotoba*), while *tama* indicates a "mystery" (*kushibi*) that is "difficult to understand by ear or grasp by hand" and that lodges in things, constituting their essence. The *tama* is further defined as "the mysterious divine spirit that is granted to people as their fundamental spirit and that represents the fundamental element of language."[16] Although it is not stated explicitly, the implication is that *kotodama* is a distinctive feature of the Japanese language only, and is not found in foreign languages. Because the *kotodama* were transmitted from the divine age, they must be sought in Old Japanese (*kogo*), not in Modern Japanese.

As mentioned above, the school of *kotodama* studies was formed by an obscure group of religious scholars. The work of Usami Keidō on the origin of language represents an application of just one part of the *kotodama* theory developed by this school. To have a full understanding of the school's inspiration, we need to consider the context under which it developed. Explication of this context provides a link to some of the Shinto-based New Religions of the twentieth century, in which vestiges of the tenets of the school of *kotodama* studies may be found.

The founder of the school of *kotodama* studies, Nakamura Takamichi, claimed to have discovered an esoteric chart, the *masumi no kagami* (mirror of clarification), that arranged the letters of the Japanese syllabary in a manner that unlocked both the mystery of the voice of the gods and the role of sound in the creation of the cosmos. He claimed that oral transmission via *kotodama* was

---

[15] Usami, *Nihon kotodama-gaku gairon*, 15, 22. Various illustrations of this method are given: for example, elucidation of German "kultur" (*kurutsūru*) (34) and English "culture" (*karutyua*) (41) and of English "house" (*hausu*), perhaps the briefest example, where its meaning is explained as "/ha/: 'a large hole'; /u/: 'to conceal oneself', and /su/: 'to gather inside'" (42).

[16] Hori, *Ongi zensho*, 1:110.

alive at the time of the transmission of the *Kojiki* (712), but out of fear that the true meaning of the *Kojiki* would not be transmitted, the principles of *kotodama* were presented in this esoteric chart and placed in an Inari shrine in Kyoto.[17] It is common to ascribe the recording of certain phrases and deity names in the *Kojiki* in *man'yōgana*, and not in Chinese characters used for their meaning alone, to the need to record accurately the sound that is the essence of *kotodama*, and not simply the meaning that could be represented by Chinese characters used as logographs. Usami also argues along these lines.[18]

The unique contribution of this school to the development of *kotodama* theory has to do with its view of the role of sound in the creation of the cosmos. Proponents of the school claimed that the ancients were aware of the power of language to act as the trigger for all phenomena. They noted that in India there was an association of wind, breath, sound, and life, and in the Judaeo-Christian bible, an association and equation of the "Word" with God. They pointed out that in Japan as well, the same sound /na/ can be found in the terms *nanoru* 'to name'; *naru* 'to become'; *naru* 'to bear'; *naru* 'to sound', 'to form'; and *nari* 'to act'. Their interpretation of sound as the creative force of the universe centered on the sound /su/, which appeared at the center of their secret chart of the Japanese syllabary. This chart included the voiced and /p/ versions of the syllabary and therefore contained what are referred to as the "seventy-five sounds." They identified the essence of the sound /su/ to be its function of unifying all things and pointed to forms such as *suberu* 'to rule' and *sumera mikoto* 'divine ruler' as indicative of this primordial function.[19] *Kotodama* for this school ultimately meant "the voice of the gods," and that voice initiating creation through sound.

Several New Religions, including the Ōmotokyō of Deguchi Onisaburō (1871–1948) and the Sūkyō Mahikari of Okada Kōtama (1901–1974), were heavily influenced by this sound-based system of cosmology and adopted it as part of their teachings.[20] Usami Keidō was a member at one time of the Ōmotokyō.

---

[17] Kaisetsu-hen, *Ōishigori Masumi zenshū*, 43.

[18] Usami, *Nihon kotodama-gaku gairon*, 45.

[19] Kaisetsu-hen, *Ōishigori Masumi zenshū*, 38, 40, 45.

[20] See Ann Wehmeyer, "The Power of the Word and Spiritual Cleansing," and also Winston Davis, *Dojo: Magic and Exorcism in Modern Japan*.

Depending on the historical period, "word spirit" has been viewed as unique to the Japanese language, and when thus construed, it constitutes part of the ideology of *Nihonjinron* (theory of Japanese uniqueness): the investigation of the cultural characteristics of the Japanese people that distinguish them from peoples of other countries or civilizations. In the work of Usami Keidō, we have seen that it is not *kotodama* itself that is unique to the Japanese language; rather, the special circumstances of the land and natural features of the Japanese archipelago have allowed "word spirit" to be harnessed in its purest form.

In conclusion, I would argue that the vestiges of *fūdo* can be seen in two areas in contemporary Japan. The first is in the tendency of cultural critics to focus on Japan as a land of "four seasons," which, it is argued, engender a culture that is more variegated, on the one hand, and more able to adopt, on the other, various alien cultural practices, which may then be modified for application to the Japanese context. This approach seems to echo in the following statement of Tada Michitarō: "The countries which have these seasons are quite few but have generally been responsible for most recent cultural history."[21]

The second area is in the promotion of regionally based production as superior, or what may be called a type of national-product fetishism. Although those in government and business circles may argue in what seems to those outside Japan to be a type of fabrication designed to engineer domestic consumption of domestically produced items, such as Japanese skiis particularly suited to the moisture of Japanese snow or Japanese rice endowed with a special flavor resulting from its growth in Japanese soil, the Japanese consumer seems more than willing to buy into the concept of the added worth of a product's being produced in Japan out of the unique environment and designed especially for Japanese tastes.

The sound symbolism of both the school of *kotodama* studies and the theory of sound-meaning school may be compared to Plato's (d. 349 B.C.) recourse to sound symbolism as the generative force underlying language in the *Cratylus*. Plato wished to reject the notion that words were established simply on the basis of human convention (*nomos*).[22] In his view, the names for things should be "correct" in that they be expressive of the essence of

---

[21] Tada Michitarō, "Japanese Sensibility," 105.
[22] See Esa Itkonen, *Universal History of Linguistics*, 167ff.

things. The origin of words should therefore, in some sense, be natural (*phusis*), rather than arbitrary. The onomatopoetic theory of the origin of language is considered and rejected in the *Cratylus*, and the conclusion is that, in the beginning, there was an ultimate "name-giver," who created words by using the sounds most expressive of the nature of the thing being named.[23]

Both in Plato and in the two Japanese schools, the origin of language is assumed to lie in sound symbolism, at the level of phonemes or syllables. Also common to both is the idea that something beyond human convention has had a role in linking human vocal sounds to the representation of things. What is unique to the school of *kotodama* studies is the notion that the particular climatic conditions of Japan have allowed for the essence of things to be expressed in the purest form. Usami's theory appeared just at the time when national characteristics of the Japanese were beginning to be linked to geographical features and just at the end of the work by the theory of sound-meaning school. Accordingly, the times were ripe for just such an interface of the two constructs of *kotodama* and *fūdo*.

References

Akimoto Kichirō. 1993. Kaisetsu. In *Fudoki*, ed. Akimoto Kichirō, in *Nihon koten bungaku taikei (NKBT)*, shinsōhan, 7–31. Tokyo: Iwanami Shoten.

Aoki Michiko Yamaguchi, trans. 1971. *Izumo fudoki*. Tokyo: Sophia University.

Bellah, Robert N. 1965. Japan's cultural identity: Some reflections on the work of Watsuji Tetsuro. *Journal of Asian Studies* 24, 4 (1965): 573–594.

Brown, Roger. 1958. *Words and things*. Glencoe, Ill.: Free Press.

Dale, Peter N. 1986. *The myth of Japanese uniqueness*. New York: St. Martin's Press.

Davis, Winston. 1980. *Dojo: Magic and exorcism in modern Japan*. Stanford, Calif.: Stanford University Press.

Dilworth, David. 1974. Watsuji Tetsurō (1889–1960): Cultural phenomenologist and ethician. *Philosophy East and West* 24, 1 (January 1974): 3–22.

---

[23] H. N. Fowler, *Plato, With an English Translation*, 145ff.

Fowler, H. N. 1926. *Plato, with an English translation.* Vol. 6: *Cratylus, Parmenides, Greater Hippias, Lesser Hippias.* London: William Heinemann.
Hori Hidenari. 1913. *Ongi zenshū,* ed. Jingū hōsaikai. Posthumous works; 2 vols. Tokyo: Jingū Hōsaikai.
Itkonen, Esa. 1991. *Universal history of linguistics: India, China, Arabia, Europe.* Amsterdam/Philadelphia: John Benjamins.
Kindaichi Kyōsuke. 1992. Kotodama o megurite. In *Kindaichi Kyōsuke zenshū.* Vol. 1: *Gengogaku,* ed. Kindaichi Kyōsuke zenshū henshū i'inkai, 240–265. Tokyo: Sanseidō.
Levy, Ian Hideo. 1980. *The ten thousand leaves.* Princeton, N.J.: Princeton University Press.
Minami Hiroshi. 1980. *Nihonjinron no keifu.* Tokyo: Kōdansha gendai shinsho.
Nagami Isamu. The ontological foundation in Tetsurō Watsuji's philosophy: *Kū* and human existence. *Philosophy East and West* 31, 3 (July): 279–296.
Najita, Tetsuo, and H. D. Harootunian. 1988. Japanese revolt against the West: Political and cultural criticism in the twentieth century. In *The Cambridge history of Japan.* Vol. 6: *The twentieth century,* ed. Peter Duus, 711–774. Cambridge: Cambridge University Press.
Ōishigori Masumi. 1981. *Ōishigori Masumi zenshū.* 3 vols. and Kaisatsu-hen. Fujisawa City, Kanagawa Prefecture: Ōishigori Masumi zenshū kankōkai/Tokyo: Yawata Shoten.
Seeley, Christopher. 1991. *A history of writing in Japan.* Leiden: E. J. Brill.
Tada Michitarō. 1985. Japanese sensibility: An "imitation" of Yanagita. In *International perspectives on Yanagita Kunio and Japanese folklore studies,* ed. J. Victor Koschmann, Ōiwa Keibō, and Yamashita Shinji, 97–120. Ithaca, N.Y.: East Asia Program, Cornell University.
Takagi Ichinosuke, Gomi Tomohide, and Ōno Susumu, eds. *Man'yōshū.* In *NKBT,* vols. 4–7. Tokyo: Iwanami Shoten.
Toyoda Kunio. 1980. *Nihonjin no kotodama shisō.* Tokyo: Kōdansha.
Usami Keidō. 1976. *Nihon kotodama-gaku gairon.* Nagoya: Reikyō Sanbō. Originally appeared in *Nihon oyobi Nihonjin,* January 1932.
Watsuji Tetsurō. 1961. *Climate and culture: A philosophical study by Watsuji Tetsurō.* Trans. Geoffrey Bownas. Tokyo: Ministry of Education/Hokuseido Press.

———. 1975 printing. *Fūdo: Ningenteki kōsatsu*. Tokyo: Iwanami Shoten, 1935.

Wehmeyer, Ann. 1991. The concept of *kotodama* in Edo period nativism. *Annals*, Southeast Conference, Association for Asian Studies, 13:71–80.

———. 1995. The power of the word and spiritual cleansing: *Kotodama* ('word spirit') in the Shinji Shūmeikai, a New Religion in Japan. Paper presented at the Southeast Conference, Association for Asian Studies, Hilton Head, South Carolina, January.

EIGHT

Modern Roots in Ancient Traditions:
Pilgrimage on Mount Fuji

ERIK L. MOORE

The role of the pilgrim is a role of transformation. As a person steps out of the flow of everyday life and takes on a new mantle, a new character is created. The person lives by new precepts, new goals, and in constantly changing surroundings during the pilgrimage. Even after the ritual, as the person returns to the previous environment, the new self takes back with it the personal experiences of the pilgrim. Identity is transformed in the light of these experiences by incorporating newly acquired perspectives. This transformation occurs in societies all over the world, such as the Hadj in the Arab world, pilgrimages to Jerusalem in Christendom, the Walkabout of Australia, the trip to Bodh Gaya in the Buddhist world, and the trek of the pilgrims or *junreisha* up Fujisan in Japan.

My reason for making the pilgrimage up Fujisan was a desire for personal transformation through an "inward journey" on this mountain. By "inward journey," I mean a period of reflection, meditation, and self-analysis, which involves time away from those routine schedules, social relationships, and material attachments that hold us in particular roles and ways of thinking. Leaving these attachments to go on a pilgrimage offers some space for the reevaluation of one's assumptions, goals, and habits. Personal identity becomes amorphous as it is removed from the environment that shapes it. The outward role of the pilgrim, the symbolism of the rituals, and the strenuous nature of the physical journey together offer new perspective and give fresh context to the past.

Unless these new perspectives and insights are applied to life after the ritual, the journey is meaningless. The pilgrimage offers a space and time in which to incorporate changes into one's personal perspectives, an opportunity to grow. It offers a milestone from which to set a new course for identity. This is the transformation I was looking for.

I picked Fujisan for my pilgrimage because my wife is Japanese and I have empathized with many rituals, places, and people in Japan during the time I have spent there. Fujisan is the ultimate landmark of Japanese identity, and it became an obvious focus of my empathy. Its virtual omnipresence on the horizon of the region of Japan with the largest population earns it the status of national icon. But the way in which I identify my experiences in Japan with Fujisan perhaps reveals the stereotypes that I bring with me as a foreigner.

My success on this journey would, in part, be based on my ability to enter the role of the pilgrim with authenticity. I would depend greatly on the traditions and people with whom I would come into contact. Were their traditions permeable enough to receive me, an obvious foreigner, into their rituals? Would I be able to perform the role of the pilgrim with credibility? This pilgrimage was to become not only a challenge for me, but also a test of the openness of the traditions of Fujisan.

Konohanasakuya-hime was a Japanese princess seeking eternal life through her legendary journey up Fujisan.[1] The metaphor of this princess' quest for eternal life applies directly to the inward solitary journey of the pilgrim climbing the mountain, looking for unchanging truths as the fleeting, transient world floats by like the *ukiyo* (floating world) of Buddhist tradition. For me this inward quest for unchanging realities relates directly to a mantra or chant used by the pilgrims of Fujisan: *Rokkon shojo, oyama wa seiten*, which means "away with the six evils, good weather on the mountain." The six evils are thought by people who live on the mountain to be of Buddhist origin and refer to the five senses and will. The turning away from the senses demonstrates the desire to focus on internal ideas and identity rather than on external cues as perceived through the senses. Looking inside to seek universal and unchanging truths is not unlike the quest for eternal life. The wish for good weather, by contrast, is thought to apply more directly to the harsh environment of Fujisan, so it represents a more practical wish of the traveler.

My own pilgrimage up the mountain had as much to do with the desire for the experience of an inward journey as it did with

---

[1] The Mt. Fuji Wilderness Park Society, *Handbook for Climbing Mount Fuji* (Tokyo, 1992), 15.

an empathy for the traditions of the area and a desire to participate in its rituals. Therefore my first task was to find out the "right way" to perform the pilgrimage. I felt it was necessary to define as many rituals with as much detail as possible so that I would be able to participate in the authentic and complete process. I consulted with many Japanese friends and relied heavily on my wife's family to help me research the appropriate clothing, rituals, accessories, and plan of action. Through participation in the rituals, I was determined to make this inward journey.

Preparation for the Trip

I learned that the clothing of pilgrims on Fuji should be white. When I asked a worker in a shrine at the fifth station of Fuji why this was, he laughed and said it was more for the ease of spotting lost pilgrims than it was to demonstrate sacredness. The first time I heard this, I was startled by what struck me as the audacity of the priest, but his comment revealed a perspective of warm familiarity with the tradition that did not deny or desecrate its spiritual value. The shoes should be *jikatabi*, a two-toed shoe with a thin rubber sole well suited to rock climbing. In modern Japan, such shoes are most commonly worn by gardeners and construction workers, but their *tabi* are usually black; white ones are rare. Between the *jikatabi* and the bottom of the pants are white cloth leg wrappings called *kyahan*, which keep the dirt out. Each hand is covered with a cloth *tekkou*, which wraps around the wrist and follows the back of the hand, attaching to the middle finger with a string loop. It protects the hand and fingers from insects at low altitudes and from sun and wind at higher elevations. The pants, buttoned tight along the calves, are baggy at the thighs, allowing for ventilation. An apron or *maekake* with many pockets for keeping things handy is worn over the lap. The hat or *sugegasa* is wide brimmed and made of straw, large enough to keep the sun and rain off the face, neck, and shoulders, yet not so large that one is blown off the mountain. As I was climbing to the seventh station, a fellow wearing the same kind of hat warned me not to tie the string around my neck but to tie it double around my chin so that I wouldn't be choked in a gust of wind.

The pilgrim carries various items that are useful on the trek up the mountain. The staff or *kongozue* (one translation of *kongozue* is "the staff of Herculean power," which every pilgrim can surely use on Fujisan) is not only an aid to climbing and walking but is also the place where the hot brands are recorded at each rest station of the mountain. Shrines record their mark on the staff with a red stamp hammered into the wood. Bells are also hung from the staff, a tradition that seems to have multiple sources. Some say the bells are to alert the *kami* (gods) on the mountain to your presence, as in the Shinto shrine tradition. Others say that it is the Buddhist tradition of making noise to warn little animals to flee lest they be stepped on. As with the white clothes, the shrine workers of Fujisan joke that it is to find lost pilgrims. A blue shoulder bag or *sanyabukuro* with a book serves to record the seals and inscriptions of each shrine along the path; I used this book also as a journal. Pilgrims who chant also generally need a string of beads called a *juzu* to keep track of the chanting. Sometimes I had to put mine away when I was climbing particularly steep paths and needed my hands to grab the face of the mountain. Like most other pilgrims, I also opted for a backpack filled with nonspecialized travel supplies such as a warm coat, water, maps, camera, and the like.

The Journey

Equipped in this way, I plunged into the pilgrimage with beads in hand and the mantra in my mind. I had fulfilled all the standard ritualistic preparations I was aware of save one: I was not a native Japanese. At first this obvious fact had not occurred to me, but as I began the preparations, Japanese and Americans occasionally expressed skepticism concerning my motives, questioned the validity of a foreigner's performing this ritual, explored the sincerity of my efforts, or even proposed the possible sacrilege I could be invoking on the experience. I decided to let the experience itself provide the resolution of these questions. It is true that I was not raised in Japan, nor with my blue eyes and blond hair will I ever be mistaken for a Japanese on sight, but I would perform this ritual, allow it to transform me, and see how permeable Fujisan's traditions could be.

My journey took its formal start in Shibuya, where I caught the first train on the way to Fujisan. In this location where foreigners are common and New Religion people dressed in white are always bothering passersby, my role as a pilgrim was only an internal thought. To the people of Shibuya, I was an oddity to be grouped with the other strangelings seen there daily. With such a beginning, I began to question the validity of my trip. Were the traditional roles of this island so impregnable that I could not transform myself within their boundaries?

As I transferred at Tokyo Station, some other pilgrims got off the train on their return trip. They greeted me warmly and gave good reports of weather. They seemed not to notice my Caucasian face as they shared a snatch or two of their experiences. These were the first people I had met who were also participating in the rituals of Fujisan, and the immediate warm rapport, however brief, was a welcome change.

Upon arriving in Fujiyoshida, on the north side of Fujisan, I was greeted at the door of the Yoshida-ya Ryokan, a small inn in the center of the city, by the caretaker, who was amazed at my garb and ability, limited though it was, to speak Japanese. She showed me to my room and recommended where to get food and supplies for the climb. After the evening bath, I talked with her and her daughter for several hours about the customs of the mountain, climbing conditions, and my reasons for climbing. She introduced me to several customs, including the appropriate gates or *torii* through which to make my approach to the mountain. The next morning she sent me on my way and returned part of the fee for the night's lodging as a gesture of support for my pilgrimage. Her support in money and personal interest demonstrated that I had at least begun the transition to a role within her tradition.

This all came as a pleasant surprise because my wife had called many an inn in the city hoping to place me for the night and had been turned down as soon as the innkeepers heard my foreign last name. Even the *ryokan* where I eventually stayed refused at first to have me. As my wife pressed further, this innkeeper revealed her assumptions about foreigners: she thought they would be rude, speak no Japanese, and be unable to bathe or eat properly. I had to overcome these stereotypes before I could enter into her tradition. Perhaps the hardest stereotype to overcome is that foreigners do outlandish things. "Playing the pilgrim" could easily have been outlandish in her mind, yet "being the pilgrim" invoked a different response.

Walking from the inn in the morning, I began to turn inward. Except for the occasional group of children attracted to me, I walked unnoticed. As I reached the edge of town I found the Kitaguchi Sengenjinja, a shrine that forms the Northern Gate to the mountain, where I met another climber. He was a mountain climber, not a pilgrim, but together we performed the rituals of purification before climbing the mountain. We washed our faces, hands, and mouths in the water provided at the front of the shrine. We drank sake from a small plate at the shrine, and I bought the staff I was to lean on during the climb. With all due veneration, the priest at the shrine hammered the red temple stamp into it for me and then put the shrine seal and script into my record book.

While at the shrine, I noticed that the priests' everyday functions were to bless the cars and trucks of the local people, perform baby-naming ceremonies, and carry out other civic duties. I had expected to see more pilgrims in the height of climbing season, July 30, but there was only a meager trickle on this day. The day I was there, the priest and I seemed to be the only ones keeping the tradition of the pilgrimage alive. The traveler I met there confessed that he would not have performed the rituals if I had not been there. He had climbed many mountains in Japan, and although Fujisan was important because it was the country's highest peak, it was more a casual hobby than a ritual climb for him. It was also apparent from the small number of staves for sale there that few people now start out on a formal journey from this historical point of entry into the mountain. After passing into the forest on the north slope of Fujisan, we didn't see anyone for hours except the occasional construction truck. There were no clear signs leading to the footpath we would take to the top. Even with a map, we had great difficulty keeping to the path. One concern about Fujisan is that compasses do not work on the mountain because of the large magnetic mineral deposits in the region, so people often get lost. Adding to these concerns were rumors we had both heard that the woods at the foot of Fuji are used by people wishing to commit suicide. We were hoping not to come across any horrific scenes or crazed suicidal person with a gun. After an hour or so, though, we reached the way station Nakanochaya, a sure sign we were on the right path.

In Nakanochaya the virtual abandonment of Fujisan's tradition became apparent. Although there were a few small newer monuments, the huge old stone monuments and buildings were in disrepair. It was like a forgotten graveyard. It seems that pilgrims frequented this way so rarely that the shrines and way stations along it had long been abandoned.

The next main stop from Nakanochaya is Ichigome, the first of ten main stations leading to the rim of the volcano I knew as Fujisan. It was even more of a ghost town, though with a path still running through it. The abandonment of these shrines and stations indicates a turning away from the traditions that built and sustained them over the years. Considering the status of Fujisan as a symbol of Japanese national identity, this seemed almost impossible to me at the time. There was the same sense of devastation as I continued on the trail through the first five stations. Only rarely was there evidence that some shrines were still being maintained and venerated. These few were caged by tall metal security fences that seemed to entrap the shrines more than protect them.

The desolation and neglect made it seem as if a part of the Japanese identity was dying. Most of the people who had used the pilgrimage from the Northern Gate as a catalyst for change in their lives had long since given up this ritual. The families that had maintained these traditions for generations had turned to other things. The shrines were being lost to the vines and the dust, and the rituals performed in them were surely likewise being forgotten. I began to feel that I was trying to grow roots in long-barren soil. Before beginning my journey I had been concerned about finding a tradition permeable enough to enter, but instead I was finding this tradition decaying. It wasn't until I reached the New Fifth Station that I understood why these practices had been given up.

As the slope steepened, I began noticing bits of garbage bags, aluminum cans, and cardboard boxes in the streambeds. The trash had apparently washed down to this elevation during rainstorms. As we approached the main road leading to the New Fifth Station, we came across a small shrine—no bigger than a small toolshed—that was very well taken care of. It seemed to be a shrine dedicated to the garbage. Just above this shrine of the tainted forest we stepped out into a view like a strip mine. Huge retaining walls crisscrossed the slopes, and large troughs directed sliding rock. Wire mesh and rock created barriers to direct the natural flow of the volcanic cinders. Fujisan was being shaped by earthmoving equipment to make it safe for the supply vehicles that serviced the New Fifth Station and above.

The way we had climbed the mountain was now the back entrance. We had come through the veritable garbage dump of the New Fifth Station. This new station is akin to a small Disneyland. It is perched on a prominence of the mountain that is part of an earlier eruption than that which created the familiar mountain we know today. This is why it is stable, and both safer from landslides and easier to build on than other parts of the mountain.

As I entered the asphalt parking lot of the New Fifth Station, I experienced a kind of culture shock similar to what must have happened to people coming from the Tokugawa period into the Meiji industrial revolution. It was as though a culture completely different from that which had built the old stations below had constructed the new station.

This new world seemed at first to be devoid of the old traditions. The dominant group was tourists who arrived on luxury buses from ports of call such as Shinjuku. For them there was no time for the transformation of identity that could take place during the longer walk up from the Northern Gate. They could come out in the morning from Tokyo in comfort and be herded by a tour guide up the mountain. These tourists were insulated from individual decisions about where to go, what to do, and even what to think. All the answers were provided by the guide. The thought of participating in rituals with any sense of depth was far from the minds of these modern-age sightseers.

What was lacking in this new breed of travelers was the possibility of facing the journey in a way that would allow them to step outside their habitual personae. Generally, they travel in groups from their hometowns or schools. There is not the same predisposition toward inward reflection provided in the pilgrim's role. Their experience is surely valid and rewarding, but the contemplative options seem to be overlooked on the New Fifth Station. The consolation prize is a shopping spree in the host of gift shops.

As these tourists responded to me, they seemed to echo the comments I experienced in Shibuya. Polite tourists mentioned that I had nice clothes and asked why a foreigner was wearing such traditional clothes. It was usually not in their realm of possibilities that I could actually be a real pilgrim performing the rituals with authenticity. Younger tourists just yelled out *"Henna gaijin,"* not in an intentionally negative way, but with amusement and amazement at "what those crazy foreigners do." *Gaijin* means "foreigner" or "outsider." There were plenty of these on the mountain, but they could be discounted as tourists not really participating in any Japanese traditions. *Henna* means "strange." What was strange about me was my invasion of Japanese traditions. If my eyes had been like theirs and my hair darker, those youths likely would have found me boring or passé.

I did find a few pilgrims in the New Fifth Station. It seemed that many pilgrims now take the bus up the mountain and start their journey from there. Some of them wear the traditional clothing, some wear only the *jikatabi*, and others just wear white clothes in the modern Western style. Whenever I met people who were on Fujisan for inner reasons, they seemed to have worked out their own traditions. They picked the rituals that were important to them and often made up other rituals to perform to make their experiences on the mountain special. They seemed to be in personal control of their identity and not confined by any set of rules.

From here, I went on to the Sixth Station. There I would stay the night with the Sasuga family, who run the station, called Unkaiso (The Sea of Clouds) because it is at such an elevation that often the tops of the clouds are at your feet, as though you could jump in and swim. They immediately invited me into their living quarters and treated me to dinner, which was not easy for them considering I am vegetarian. We talked for hours late into the evening debating the meaning of Fujisan's mantra, explaining our personal philosophical beliefs, and considering the drastic changes that had taken place on the mountain over the past few years. The patriarch of the family was referred to as *Fujisan sensei* or the teacher of Fujisan. I called him Sasuga-san. As we were eating, NHK radio called him for an interview. They call him every day during the climbing season to get reports on the weather or interesting events for their news broadcasts. He asked me to be interviewed, and I tried to explain to them why I was climbing, but I'm not sure they ever understood my explanation, partly because of my limited Japanese.

Sasuga-san did not espouse any formal religion. He preferred Shinto to Buddhism but said that his empathy with the mountain was stronger than either of these. He venerated his father in a special place on the wall. He had inherited the mountain way station as well as many personal traditions and philosophies from his father. He claimed to be more "from the mountain" than "from Japan." Many of the tourists he saw every day from Tokyo and Niigata were more foreign to him than I was. They were from a culture alien to him, a culture that consumed his traditions like a form of entertainment instead of venerating them and preserving the rituals by participating in them. This new group, he felt, was causing the mountain to become dirty and abused. These people would throw trash carelessly, for they had lost touch with the mountain. He was the caretaker of the traditions he inherited, and they were simply the audience. As I prepared for sleep, I tried to consider the context in which this new generation of cultural consumers had risen.

Sasuga-san's identity was based on a family lineage; he had no need for national identity. His doctrines and rituals were personal, and it was his option to change them as the situation changed. His philosophy allowed him to accept me automatically as a sincere pilgrim both because there was no higher authority that needed to be consulted and because we related in a direct way. In my travels throughout Japan, I have met many people like him. My entry into their world is not disturbing because they are in control and have the ability to adapt. This type of culture is permeable because the individual is always able to respond to new individuals spontaneously instead of feeling required to judge them as potential paradoxes established by a set of group rules.

Transformation

Many tourists on Fujisan base some of their identity on nationalistic themes, such as the racial uniqueness of Japanese experience, which came out in their responses to me. They travel to popular Japanese tourist sights to understand themselves and confirm the foundations of their national identity. Any injection of foreign elements into these traditions creates contradictions that must be rejected if they are to maintain this national identity. These tourists visit people like Sasuga-san to confirm their assumptions of Japaneseness, assumptions by which he has never been restricted. He confirms these assumptions by simply being a person of the Japanese race who is obviously involved in some tradition on Fujisan, an icon of Japanese national identity. The tourists rarely make an effort to understand his traditions, his beliefs, or his predisposition toward they themselves. Because they lack direct information, they are free to use him as a confirmation of their own stereotypes, and he becomes a brick in the foundation of their sense of national identity.

These consumeristic notions of Japanese identity have a strong base in the national educational system. I explored the structure and content of Japanese junior high school and high school students by interviewing many Japanese college students at Teikyo Loretto Heights University, where I teach. I found that the heavy dose of moral lessons and of Japanese history that they receive often bonds them together in some ways as patriots of Japan. This building of national identity through the educational system is not unique to Japan. However, one special characteristic of the Japanese system is that it does not teach self-determinism or critical thinking. As Karl van Wolferen confirms, the education system is trying to create a docile, united population, dependent on authority to define individual identity and assumptions of homogeneity that predispose unity.[2] It is with this same set of assumptions that many Japanese tourists show up on Fujisan looking for confirmation of their indoctrinated national identity. If they happen to run into me, I create a paradox. As a foreigner, I cannot merge with their national homogeneity, nor am I subject to their authorities. Therefore I cannot be a serious part of the traditions in their mind and must be labeled as *henna gaijin*, an otherwise unexplainable exception. This sense of cultural identity creates an insular group with which I could never hope to merge, even through the transformation of pilgrimage. For me, this national culture is impermeable.

Yet in many and various ways, all Japanese are similar to Sasuga-san. When they rely on personal experience, they happily contradict the national propaganda of Japaneseness. It is mainly in those areas in which they lack direct experience or are unable to focus critical attention that they defer to the clichés of national identity.

As I climbed the next morning, I met several people like Sasuga-san on the path to the rim: pilgrims, priests at the shrines, or other kinds of shrine workers, though the tourists far outnumbered them. Many foreigners were also climbing Fujisan: those who were working in Japan, people visiting for a week or two, and mountain climbers from all over the world. The other foreigners fit more easily than I did into the Japanese nationalistic mind-set. These people were clearly defined as tourists and were comfortably external to the traditions.

When I reached the edge of the rim, I had my staff stamped with the shrine stamp and had its seal and inscription entered into my book. Then I set off along the rim. I went around the crater to Fuji Radar, where the highest point in the rim creates the true peak of Fujisan. Here I found a group of middle-aged businessmen who had been climbing the mountain every year since their high school days. We spoke a while, and I watched as they wrote

---

[2] *The Enigma of Japanese Power* (New York: Random House, 1990), chap. 4.

poems in traditional calligraphy to hang on the walls of their homes for the coming year. They preferred high-tech sports clothes to the traditional pilgrim clothes. They were making their own tradition on the mountain.

I stayed the night in a mountain hut on the Gotenba side of the rim. There I met a Japanese television crew who found me interesting and arranged to interview me the next day at sunrise. Some of the footage ended up on an NHK special about Fujisan shown at New Year's. I ended up among some other video clips of foreigners as a three-second sound bite, stating that I was a pilgrim. I suppose that I was a *henna gaijin* more than anything else in that show.

Viewing the sunrise is perhaps the most nationalistic of all rituals on the rim. Two of the strongest symbols of Japan are Fujisan and the rising sun, so these must of course be melded into a singular experience for the tourist. Tourists are carefully herded up the mountain with a keen sense of timing to see the sun rise on the Fujiyoshida side of the rim (where trinket stands abound) as music blares from loudspeakers. When the moment finally arrives, crowds of tourists, carefully directed by their leaders, yell *Banzai!* in honor of the sunrise. As I went to meet the TV crew, I passed by a group of about twenty Japanese tourists. They all gawked at me and asked the tour guide to explain who I was. He was at a complete loss. For him, I was surely a paradox. His understanding of the traditions of the pilgrimage on Fujisan must have been based on a national, and thus racial, sense of identity.

After the interview, I headed back around the rim to the Fujinomiya side. I met up with a couple who were stacking rocks, one on top of the other. They explained that it was from a Buddhist notion: in one particular hell people are required to stack a thousand rocks one on top of the other to obtain relief from their suffering. In this world we can stack up a few rocks and do them a favor by getting them started. The people I spoke with denied having any religious faith in the story; they were just leaving a mark on the mountain inasmuch as they had come all the way up. They were making their own personal traditions by transforming the traditional ones.

Conclusion

I began to understand that my goal of climbing Fujisan the "right way" was not possible, not because the traditional shrines had fallen into ruin, but because there is no one right way. The insular, nationalistic notions of climbing Fujisan are only the superficial stereotypes of the inward traditions of the pilgrimage. People seeking the inward path from different backgrounds, especially the ones from around Fujisan, modify the traditions they inherit to fit their own needs. The only "right way" I would find on the mountain would be the "right way for me at that time." This type of flexible ritual with a variety of possible meanings and origins is found in other places in Japan,[3] and surely the whole world. It is more than a permeable tradition. It reaches out for anyone willing to share in it, in any way possible.

The next group I came across—about fifteen Japanese people in modern clothing intently focused on praying before a *torii* just south of the main shrines facing Fujiyoshida—seemed insular at first. They had just placed food in front of the *torii*, so I decided to take a picture of them. As I did this, they caught sight of me and came over to talk to me. They invited me to participate in their ceremony and had me face them, sitting in front of the torii as they performed some chanting and gestures over me. They had me drink a concoction that seemed to be a sake base with herbs in it. When they were done, they thanked me and seemed pleased with themselves. We had shared a very personal ritual and then taken lots of pictures. As I was leaving, they took all the food from in front of the *torii* and stuffed it into my backpack despite my objections. I felt I had imposed on them by interrupting their activities, and yet their rituals were spontaneous enough to enwrap me and create a new experience—something that enriched each of us, despite our divergent backgrounds. These people were not hindered from sharing with me by some national identity that needed to be maintained. Their sense of identity was internally driven, making their group permeable enough to reach out and share with me. Through pilgrimage we were able to transform not only ourselves, but the very rituals we shared.

It is the space of the mountain that allows room for such dramatic transformations of the identity of individuals. Here, high above the social restrictions of Japanese society, people seem

---

[3] Richard K. Beardsley, John W. Hall, and Robert E. Ward, *Village Japan* (Chicago: University of Chicago Press, 1959), 464–46.

to have more room to define themselves spontaneously. Though Fujisan is an icon of Japanese national identity, climbing it allows people to reach beyond the restrictions of that identity. As in Hokusai's thirty-six views of Fujisan, when we see the landmark of Fuji we know we are in Japan. Yet upon the mountain itself, this landmark is invisible, and the individual must seek new landmarks for personal identity.

Glossary

banzai! 万歳
Fujinomiya 富士宮
Fujisan 富士山
Fujisan Sensei 富士山先生
Fujiyoshida 富士吉田
Gotenba 御殿場
henna gaijin 変な外人
Ichigome 一合目
jikatabi 地下足袋
junreisha 巡礼者
juzu 数珠
kami 神
Kitaguchi Sengenjinja 北口浅間神社
kongozue 金剛杖
Konohanasakuya-hime 本花咲耶姫
kyahan きゃはん
maekake 前掛
nakanochaya 中ノ茶屋
Rokkon shojo, oyama wa seiten. 六根渚浄お山は晴天。
sanyabukuro さんや袋
sugegasa 菅笠
tekkou 手甲
torii 鳥居
ukiyo 浮世
Unkaiso 雲海荘
Yoshida-ya Ryokan 吉田屋旅館

Modern Roots in Ancient Traditions

Photo Captions

P. 122: Even at the summit of Mount Fuji there are organized tours of tens, hundreds, even thousands of people from all over Japan and indeed all over the world with professional tour guides. This guide is explaining to his group what I am doing there. He didn't ask me any questions before he started his explanation and assumed that I spoke no Japanese.

The people from the big cities assumed I was just some foreigner having a good time wearing the "funny clothes" of their ancestors, not part of the tradition. The participants in the living tradition readily accepted me as one of them, however, and appreciated my participation in their practices as a sincere pilgrim. It seemed strange that those from Tokyo, entering traditions about which they knew very little, disdained me, while the caretakers of those traditions readily accepted me.

P. 123: Because the direct bus service from Shinjuku Station in Tokyo is so convenient, many Japanese people start their pilgrimages at the New Fifth Station rather than hiking the traditional route. These women were pleased to see me, asked me about my clothing and hat, and wanted to see all my accessories. They were having fun hiking the mountain together, but this was also a pilgrimage for them.

I parted company with my mountain-climber acquaintance here. He was eager to climb, while I wanted to go more slowly and experience the more traditional activities.

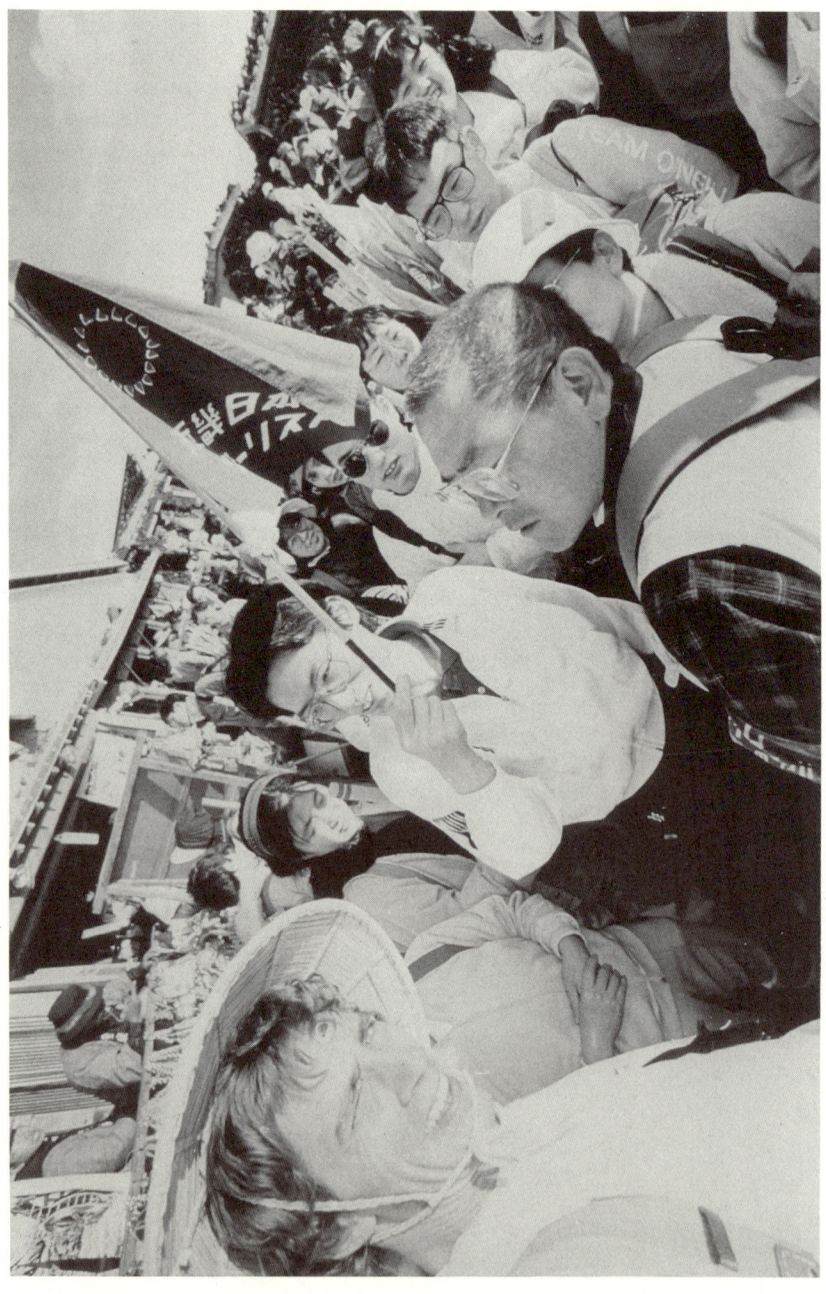

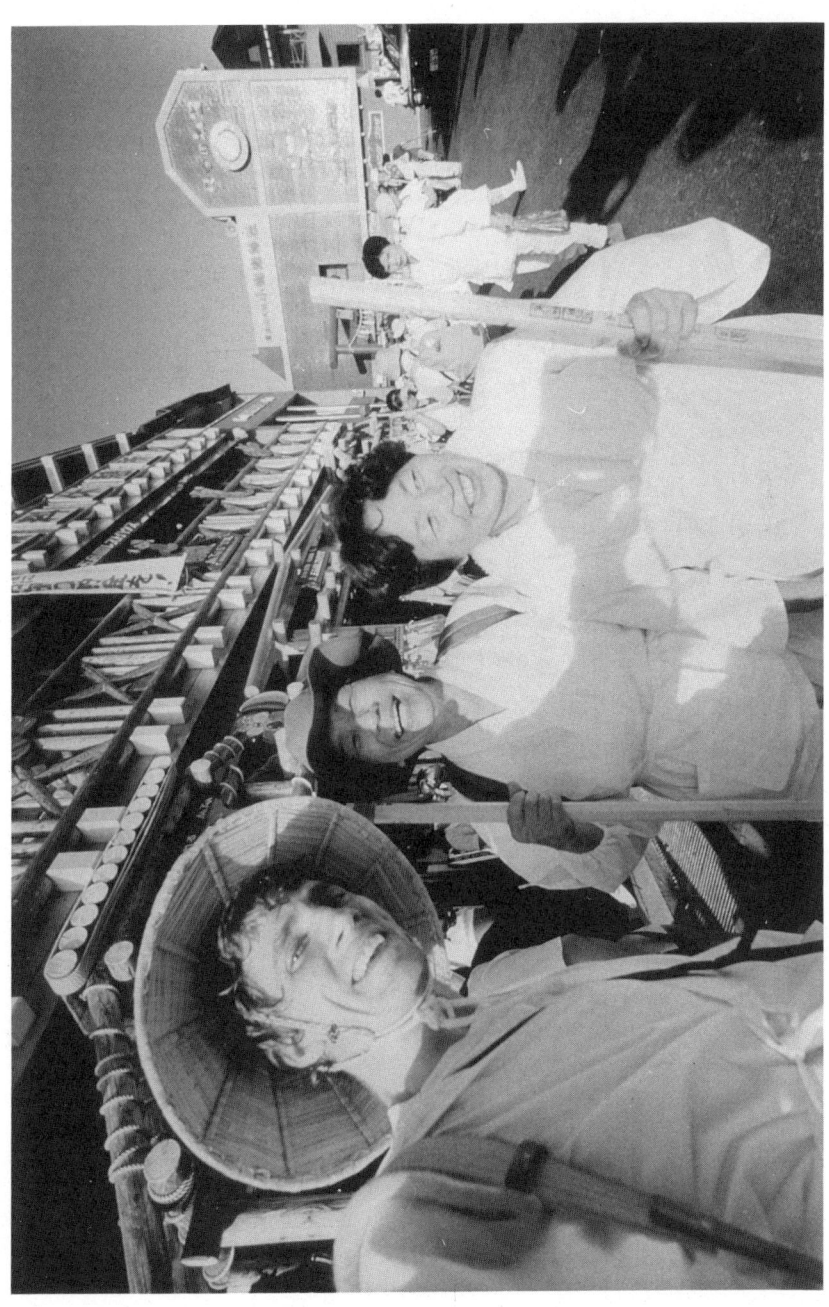